SPARKS OFF THE MAIN STRIKE

other books by the author

POETRY

Dawn Visions
Burnt Heart/Ode to the War Dead
This Body of Black Light Gone Through the Diamond
The Desert is the Only Way Out
The Chronicles of Akhira
The Blind Beekeeper
Mars & Beyond
Laughing Buddha Weeping Sufi
Salt Prayers
Ramadan Sonnets
Psalms for the Brokenhearted
I Imagine a Lion
Coattails of the Saint
Abdallah Jones and the Disappearing-Dust Caper
Love is a Letter Burning in a High Wind
The Flame of Transformation Turns to Light
Underwater Galaxies
The Music Space
Cooked Oranges
Through Rose Colored Glasses
Like When You Wave at a Train and the Train Hoots Back at You
In the Realm of Neither
The Fire Eater's Lunchbreak
Millennial Prognostications
You Open a Door and it's a Starry Night
Where Death Goes
Shaking the Quicksilver Pool
The Perfect Orchestra
Sparrow on the Prophet's Tomb
A Maddening Disregard for the Passage of Time
Stretched Out on Amethysts
Invention of the Wheel
Sparks Off the Main Strike

THEATER / THE FLOATING LOTUS MAGIC OPERA COMPANY

The Walls Are Running Blood
Bliss Apocalypse

PROSE

Zen Rock Gardening
The Little Book of Zen
Zen Wisdom

SPARKS OFF THE MAIN STRIKE

POEMS

May 24 – January 10, 2009

DANIEL ABDAL-HAYY MOORE

The Ecstatic Exchange
2010
Philadelphia

Sparks Off the Main Strike
Copyright © 2010 Daniel Abdal-Hayy Moore
All rights reserved.
Printed in the United States of America

For quotes any longer than those for critical articles and reviews, contact:
The Ecstatic Exchange,
6470 Morris Park Road, Philadelphia, PA 19151-2403
email: abdalhayy@danielmoorepoetry.com

First Edition
ISBN: 978-0-578-07145-9 (paper)
Published by *The Ecstatic Exchange*,
6470 Morris Park Road, Philadelphia, PA 19151-2403

Also available from The Ecstatic Exchange:
Knocking from Inside, poems by Tiel Aisha Ansari

Original Book design by Ian Whiteman
Cover collage by the author
Back cover photograph by Omar Mullick

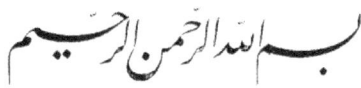

DEDICATION

To
Shaykh ibn al-Habib
(and the continuation of the Habibiyya)
Shaykh Bawa Muhaiyuddeen,
all shuyukh of instruction and ma'arifa
(and in memory of Shaykh Mansur Escudero)
and to
Baji Tayyaba Khanum
of the unsounded depths

———

*The earth is not bereft
of Light*

CONTENTS

Let The Magician   11
The Large Caster of Nets   12
Meaning   13
Soap Bubble   14
Chair   16
Crimson and Scarlet Rivulet Passageways   17
Pearl   19
A Secret Rent in the World   21
Backbent Scribes   23
And Why?   25
All Those Poets   26
Sound the Alarm   27
Skin Deep   29
Secretary Bird   31
In Broad Daylight   33
Locks on Doors   35
The Why and the Wherefore   38
Death Flips a Coin   40
19th Poem: The Projector's Beam of Light   44
The Sabotage of the Saboteurs   46
This World   48
Superhighway   49
The Pine Barrens   51
The Ship's Captain   53
Death Sonnet   55
One Shout   56
Keyhole   57
Incendiary Air   60
Treatise on Distortion   62

Deepmost Heartbeat of the World   67
Conch Shell   69
There's a Sound   71
Eon after Eon   74
Shadowhood   76
Appearance of the Muse   78
Hounds   80
Whitman   82
Little Door in the Heart   83
If Our Days are Numbered   85
Seeking and Finding   88
Lucerne Street at Night   89
The Heavenly Door That is Always Open   91
This Plane's Full of Babies   94
As We Fly Forward   95
Paradise Gate   98
Bread Was Butter and Butter Bread   100
The Doctor's Arrived   101
Stops   103
Orpheus at Rest   104
The Desperados   106
Beginnings and Endings   109
Old Man in a Drop of Water   111
Divine Name   113
Until Cockcrow Wake Us   116
The Threshold of the Floor   119
The Oyster is in Deep Meditation   121
Blind Samson   123
Love's Up Close and Personal Conflagration   124
So Many Things to Say   127
Nothing to Do   128

We Do Things   130
One Quick Cold Night   131
Synopsis of a Nonexistent Trilogy   133
A Smattering of Conundrums   137
Nowhere Was Emptiness Unrivered   138
Living Flame   140
If I Had To Say at This Moment   142
Blindly Believing   145
Optical Illusions   149
Geese Overhead   151
The Practice of Poetry   153
I Lie Face Down   157
To the Oneness   158
To Get to Sleep   160
Silent Stones   163
Some Juggler!   164
Enter the Clowns   166
The Smell of Wet Sackcloth   167
A Shout Unheard   169
In All Oracular Song   170
From the Original   172
On Us All   174
The Divine Presence   176
One Morning   177
The Way Animals Look at Us   179
A Stone   180
Opposite to This One   181
The Grand Fête   182
Shout of Joy   185
Lovely Sexy Being   186
The Truth Is   187

Jake and the Desperados   190
Delicious Liquefaction of the Dark   195
Storms   197
Various Stories   198
Every Labyrinth   200
The Thing About Death   201
The World   202
Old Boot   204
As if a Windsock   207
When We Die   210
Sparks Off the Main Strike   211

Index of Titles   214

Likulli shaay-in ghayatun annahu Wahid
To everything is the goal to become One
— ARABIC SAYING

Not out of his bliss
    Springs the stress felt
  Nor first from heaven (and few know this)
    Swings the stroke dealt —
Stroke and a stress that stars and storms deliver...
— GERARD MANLEY HOPKINS (*The Wreck of the Deutschland*)

LET THE MAGICIAN

Let the magician put his head inside his hat and
his hat upon the table and let the

table vanish into thin air

and let the swaying elephant in the wings go also
to the Land of the Invisible Table with the

head of the magician with his hat on speaking to us

of all the things it sees and doesn't see
as the sea waves close around this

entire scene and all its seers
and drowns us in its deep sea

5/24

THE LARGE CASTER OF NETS

The large Caster of Nets stood on the
shore and cast his net so wide

whole continents fell into its mesh
their blind eyes blinkless and gaping mouths

gasping for air

The large Caster of Nets kept his stride and
threw his net out into black space and

moons caught in it rolling half-lopsided their
famous smiles and winking craters
half reflecting solar light

Galaxies were next and then the universe entire
points of it jaggedly poking through its openings

and still the Net Caster strode on
new worlds in its mind and space behind it

falling through the gaps in its web

5/24

MEANING

At the knobbly ridge
like looking across an alligator's back

down into the valley below
where smoke puffs float as if

about to speak

and a dull copper sun seems on the
verge of total tarnish and the

burnt sky dazzles

we see nothing but a landscape but it
seems to describe itself in more

symbolic terms but as symbols of what
there may be no definitive explanation

except that in our hearts we see
meaning manifest itself because from

God's point of view
all has meaning

5/26

SOAP BUBBLE

A soap bubble the size of space itself
slid over space but no one

noticed the difference

The iridescences seemed sharper
that's all

The music of the spheres slid in on all
our audio frequencies replacing the

musics we listen to and except for the
angelic coefficient now a

billion times more powerful no one
noticed the difference

The presence of a benevolent presence
nearer to everybody than their own

selves slid in behind everyone's self
and said and did things in

various harmonious fashions listening to
our own voices and hearing divine

nuances and because it was so
utterly and seamlessly complete

no one noticed the difference

No one noticed the difference when instead of
sun and moon we saw a fiery sea of

God's ocular energy flaring across space in
leonine leaps reflected in the still face of

mirror-like receptivity and silvery
baths of a sweet illumination that gives our

nights the lamp we need enough to
approach God's most intimate precincts

And space itself as glistening as a
soap bubble and music that of

distant planetary places and our

own selves now totally transformed and yet
by Merciful Compassion exactly like

ourselves at this very moment though less
violent and bad tempered but

just as miraculous

CHAIR

There's a chair that whoever sits in it
becomes less proud

Grocery bags tumble their contents
out on the ground

Buildings reflect more sunlight

There's a doorway that whoever stands in it
becomes more transparent

God's Light shines through

The rooms we go from and the rooms we
go to are the same

full of illuminated furniture and
wise beings and intelligent conversation

And whoever goes through that door
leaves all concern for this world behind

And whoever enters our rooms after
going through that door

has nothing but light in their hearts
put there from the beginning of time

which shines everywhere

CRIMSON AND SCARLET RIVULET PASSAGEWAYS

The crimson and scarlet rivulet passageways
are hollowed and resonated by the rotational alphabet

that spells out this event or that unfortunate happening
in which there are lives lost or souls gained in the

peculiarly balanced roulette

"It makes sense when you think about it"

said the worm in a little jacket
standing on a rock

"but not a lot if you don't"

The entire representational unfolding takes place
on a highly grammatical scaffolding

high above every human encampment like
Shanghai New York Delhi or Sydney

in which speaking is believing

"If everyone held their tongues in silence"
asked the intrepid aphid being milked on a leaf

*"would it all return to zero —
even our blood pulse burrowing*

back into the mist?"

There was rain everywhere
sparkling against the schist

5/29

PEARL

A pearl the size of the world rolls
continuously before me

but I know I shall never string it

Can I be blamed for wanting to see
God's Face in its luster?

There is only one as it rolls into space
increasing in beauty against the blackness

and the stars

Is it one of those divine jewels
that shrink to fit our hands

once we reach out to hold them?

If this were so
I would adorn us with its glamour

It does seem to have a kind of
window on its curve

I now know is a heavenly reflection
cast on its pearlescent surface

of dimensions graspable only in our
hearts the more we let this world's

pale lusters go

Here it is again
the subject of another poem

What had been so quiet
now made manifest

The size of the world
or greater

And in its mirror
God's Face aglitter

5/30

A SECRET RENT IN THE WORLD

By a secret rent in the world
some go out into a great white

wind that blows everywhere and in
all directions at once

and could be called the Breath of God
for those who enter it are

transported into intangible territories
and lose the face they had to gain

a face we all long for
a moon face whose only reflection through

all its gestures and articulations
is God's Light and whose

ears catch only God's words and whose
mouths only speak what's within

God's hearing

and they may never come back or may
come back utterly transformed or

exactly as they left
with no distinguishing characteristics

except simplicity of being
but if they do return it's as if

from a billion miles away beyond
earth's orbit

6/2

BACKBENT SCRIBES

An underwater oceanographer looks through his
round porthole and sees a

celestial city riding on silver clouds

An astronomer glues his eyes to a telescope's eyepiece and
sees a convoy of whales just heading out

from a lunar orbit after a meeting of the *Shoosh Clan*

I look down at this page in the
act of writing and see

millennia of backbent scribes trying to
get it down in words before it

all turns back into sugar

The downpour is ceaseless but as we
glance out through the falling strands of water we might

catch a glimpse of the pearl necklaces God
dangles down from The Beloved's neck

just near enough to earth to
entice us both forward and upward

with a glitter in our eyes only
magnified by the sights we see

A thundercloud that opens on Odin's Peak

A rainbow backdrop to all the oceans
clapping their hands for joy at God's

fishy banquet day after day

and at night when moonlight spreads its
elegant silken tablecloth out on the waves

6/3

AND WHY?

Squeezing my eyes shut for a moment
I see myself from below at

three-quarter view standing on a
ledge in brown girders and shadows

What am I doing here

and why?

6/5

ALL THOSE POETS

All those poets who lament about
this and that

bitter emotional adolescent

O God let blue sheep run among them
their necks splashed with scarlet

ready for slaughter

Let the top rock of the mountain of light
crash down next to them

And then when they grab their harps to sing
let all the birds in the world for one

moment suspend their song then
join in chorus with sonic waves undersea

And the single rose of a single flower
on a tall table in an empty room

shed its tears in a blast of noon sunlight

That we ratchet our voices ever closer to
Your realm though we be but puppies at the

legs of your lowest Throne
yearning for humanhood

SOUND THE ALARM

Sound the alarm!

The great ship of the earth
is plowing through the stars

barely able to be Emperor of Ice Cream
yet we wear gold buttons cinched

to the chin

Let Beethovianic billows roar

with beeping red lights as on a
garbage truck

The earth is cutting a major swathe
through all that is noble and

electric in the universe

to find its place in a majestic orbit
where zebras graze easily next to

crocodiles

and warriors daub their faces
with red ochre and

head out by moonlight

(*shhh!* we're stalking a neighboring

tribe

because we are the earth
puffing out our chests and

raising our spears!)

6/7

SKIN DEEP

The next curve that comes
jump on it and hold on!

No – what if the space between is
greater than my calculations?

Being brighter than sunlight
has with it a certain responsibility

But in such a glare I can
barely see the next curve coming

Yours is not to sit and reason
Yours is to accumulate your forces

Love is the ingredient the two-headed
magistrate forgot to mention

He's not from either the oldest
school nor the newest

Let me simmer here among the
rapidly turning cogs

splendid as a silver skater and more
lithe in spirit than a sea horse

If I put down my pen this
watery conversation will evaporate

A trillion horses across the plain
a trillion horse-shaped clouds in the sky

Let me navigate my poor choices
past the bulk of night's shipwreck

Let no one tell you
beauty's only skin deep

6/8

SECRETARY BIRD

I would make the noble Secretary Bird
my secretary

It would prance with avian dignity round
my room awaiting dictation

A secretary who's capable of
spanning the skies and who

already has experience of flight and
perfect landings

*(Both most important
with perfect landings a high priority)*

And a fallen feather or two for a quill —
its sibilant squawks though I

at this moment have no idea at all
of its song or call

as inspiration or irritation

*(Both most important with irritation
acting often to form the near-perfect pearl)*

The rare stature of the bird!
Long hair feathers like pens behind its

ears although in fact the word
"*secretary*" may be a French corruption of

Arabic "*saqr-et-tair*" or "*hunter bird*"
since it roams the bush and

pounces on its prey with
powerful claws

(also important with both pounce and
release indispensable

prosodic attributes!)

6/9

IN BROAD DAYLIGHT

Time won't stop time won't quit
its mill wheel keeps slopping over

Even tiny sea horses their tails
twirled around stems get older

An eventful day a dreaded event
gets inevitably closer

The edge itself *dear God* edges closer
and the winds of angels rustling along our faces

even before we contemplate its
infinite spaces

Does it go beyond heaven? Does
time exist in Paradise?

Even here there are times
when a huge block of timelessness

crashes down onto the
street we happen to be strolling on

Delicious tendrils! Festival of
Nothingness! Chatterings and delectations!

Snowy shapes in full gallop in all directions
Sunlight in the dark descending its roaring beacons

Piano runs up every key in the universe
like a trillion fingers loose on the ivories

Laughter so exalted it thins at the top
into a poignant note that vanishes in the aether

Parade of fantastic phantoms
masks of all our mortal moods on their faces

Animal totems come to life!
Panthers and moose intermingled!

Soaring birds extending eternally skyward
on blue froth wings indistinguishable from the sky

And then the laughter returns to normal
and sizzles down into silence and the

squeal of tires and the knocking of crates
and angels pass in the streets in windbreakers

hooded and slightly paranoid
and time takes up its oars and prods

turns corners continues straight coughs and
lifts its face to the stars again

in broad daylight

6/10

LOCKS ON DOORS

The locks on doors are
secondary to the doors

just as doors themselves
are secondary to hinges

But doorjambs are as if
messengers with a message

where open space is concerned
through which we may go

from darkness to light
or as many variations as

space created or uncreated allows
yet nothing at all won't do

just as with doorjambs
must come doors or at least

safe passage through them and once
doors are in place then

hinges must be there so that when we're
up against them there's at least some give

for there's nothing worse than
to be facing a door that

is in actuality a wall

Then with the door on its
hinges and in readiness to

open there's the lock whose
function more a mercy than a

miracle is if locked a
barrier that necessitates a

decoder or in the case of a
door lock a particular key

without which we
remain on one side or

the other and could just as
easily be at the bottom of the

Grand Canyon on a particularly
hot day or on a day of

snow but with no easy
egress having gotten there in our

history somehow outside the
provenance of this poem

with the great canyon walls going
straight up to heaven by day or by night

leaving no alternative but to
contemplate the blue or black starry sky and its

bearing on our now nearly
microscopic selves on this side of a

locked door that actually with the right key
fitted specifically and inserted in its

lock most sweetly and expertly
(as if by magic)

opens

                                                                              6/12

THE WHY AND THE WHEREFORE

The controversy over whether the
merry-go-round was going from right to

left or from left to right was
suddenly resolved when

angels appeared at everyone's garden gate
with expectant expressions on their

moony faces and a whispering arose
loud enough to rival the very

sea and all its inhabitants and
cleared its throat for a huge

pronouncement over the world

which shall come about in
due time

Just as whether water swirls down a
drain from left to right or from

somewhere to nowhere
on the peak of the Matterhorn or the

dusty red plains of Australia

not to mention our chubby iron-clad

elder sibling Mars

and all the others to infinite gorgeousness
strung in elliptical orbits out past

inner and outermost darkness

And each angel knows the
when and the how

O Lord
awaiting Your command

And each one knows the
why and the wherefore

6/13

DEATH FLIPS A COIN

Death flips a coin in the air
and it comes down "heads"

That's the heads of all of us
sliced off our necks folks!

Though not so "Marie Antoinette"
not so grisly

In fact as the coin goes up in
slow motion over the crowd

the sun comes out from behind its
cloud and shines a ray on it

all the way from the sun's
precincts *God bless it*

And this *florin* this 10 *drachma*
this thin tin *dinar*

suddenly explodes into a kind of
spectacular fireworks dazzling

all the poor souls gathered in the
town square for an entertainment

(*which is all of us*)

And while the sunray is focused on the
coin as it tumbles heads then

tails then heads again we see a
highly concentrated visual history

of the world of our lives of a
squirrel's habits or swans landing on a

lake or a grizzly bear in hibernation
or space exploration past our

dwindling orbit out past Pluto that
now demoted planet still swinging

valiantly through its changes

And the movie continues even as the
coin begins its slow descent still

tumbling through heads and tails in the
wide eyes of its now mesmerized

audience for whom the outcome is
so important and important it

surely is for who's made provision for
Oscar's goats or Mildred's grand kids

wiping the freshly made raspberry
jam off their faces or pressing their

school smocks

And who's thought to
make amends by speech and by

gesture for that serious breech of
etiquette two years ago or

returned the plow in better shape than
when it was borrowed back to

the Johanssons and so on and
on as the coin accelerates its fall

and people don't so much think of
these details as anticipate the

worst while passionately hoping for the
best not knowing exactly and in their

bones that the best is both outcomes and
the superlative best is God's embrace

whether in death or long life and
extended breath and the clear

dazzle of miraculous being in our
hearts' eyes with what's before and

within us at this very moment and
the very moment after it as well as

this one and *this one too* as the
coin finally comes to rest on

death's bony palm at "heads"
and all of our heads turn at

once to see the light explode into
pure beauty on every living

horizon on earth with the silhouette now
of all of us throwing off our burdens whatever

they may be to walk in sheer
jubilation into it

hands raised and
voices in unison praising it as we

go

6/20

19th POEM: THE PROJECTOR'S BEAM OF LIGHT*

I write "19" with a certain expectation of
some lovely world opening under me

I can look down into as the pen glides
and the sides of a valley smoothly

ascend as the eye travels across hedgerows and
cottages as well as cattle and crows

into a more fiery center as if the
hellish core of our very planet or

simply the lowest claustrophobic part of our
eschatological consciousness where those

flames are ever stoked and ready for the
most flammable parts of us our

dross thoughts and actions we
think we do out of sight of

His Vision

They lick there behind appearances
and are real where appearances only

appear and disappear by their very
nature while both Hell's

fiery vulcanism and Paradise's lushest gardens
whose cool and perfumed leafiness and

fresh vastness are beyond imagining
are the true landscapes all

else is stretched out across as if on
thin film with its fast frame animations

and ultimate darkening until only
the Projector's intensest beam of light

outshines everything

                                                              6/23

In my handwritten poetry notebooks I consecutively number poems as I go along)

THE SABOTAGE OF THE SABOTEURS

The sabotage of the saboteurs
and the plundering of the plunderers

as well as the plunging of the plungers
and the sugaring of the sugarers

to say nothing of the planning of the planners
as well as the prevaricating of the prevaricators

are no match on any given day or night
for the generosity of The Generous

nor the forgiving of the Forgiver
Who patiently waits at the tip end of

all our breaths for us to make a
clean break from all those things

that hinder us from being kind and
naked disinhindrancers and

uncomplicated disincomplicators
to let sunlight through from the various

cloud formations onto whatever
parcel of land we've been given to be

sole cultivators of
able to bring

our whole souls to its most fecund
cultivatoring

                                                6/28

THIS WORLD

A loaf of bread on the way out

A pair of donkey ears on the way in

A hundred bottles of beer on the wall

a billion flames descending their necks

The swans of Swan Lake rising as one

The Streetcar Named Desire picking up passengers

The current situation bifurcated in streams

This instant keeping a straight face

and moving forward

SUPERHIGHWAY

A superhighway went through the village
and the people gave up their

rural ways and all bought speedsters

How or with what doesn't matter as
most went off the road some to their

fiery deaths *alas* some into the thick woods
where they frightened the panthers

and some to perfect racing skills
so excellent they began to win prizes

Their native language became
peppered with foreign words and their

native rhythms took on a harsher beat
but where they didn't perish they succeeded

until the finish line of international races
looked positively tribal with all those

flashing white teeth in sickle moon smiles
as they hoisted the trophy and

filled it with tropical flowers

The earth turned and turned until

villages burnished and metropoli perished

What had gone up went down
New folk now wore expensive suits

No one has a monopoly on excellence
nor have we conquered innate human foolishness

And where the sacred lodge once stood
a flashy diner now stands

and the wise shaman and sage longbeard
is now that crazy old bugger in levis living in a

house made of hubcaps

And the songs of the ancestors are
drowned out by the whiz of the superhighway

But no one can even remember earlier happiness
now that everyone's happy

7/1

THE PINE BARRENS

Turn left and you're in the Pine Barrens
on limited gas

Turn right and you're on an endless plain of
layered light and angels' quadrilateral tents with their
poles entering heaven whose snowy
foundations are visible through the clouds

Turn left and you enter the thickest and
greatest industrial metropolis in the
world

Turn right and right away the dazzle of the
invisible city overwhelms you for its
towers and spires arise with the
same aspirations as yourself and its acreages of
nearly audible song continue to expand out in
every direction at once

Yet this is no simple exercise since
all are within all enfolded and the

enshrinement of any is not anywhere enough
all enwrapped in each other's blesséd being and

ultimate dissipation before the
very act of their creation leading

gloriously to a vision of their

Creator's deft fingers like divine thought in flight

fashioning the subtle and the thick
with equal equanimity and equal

love

Each sheep's ear perfect each
mosquito wing an engineering wonder

each revelation to His illuminated vouchsafed ones
a proven miracle upon miracle of delight

7/4

THE SHIP'S CAPTAIN

The ship's captain is never out of earshot of
the cries and calls of his crew

as their ship sails out under a triangular moon
on a sea whose purple is the color

of interiors of orchids
and the fluctuating light from near and

distant stars is their navigational tool
as constellations map out their route

through mythic sky onto shores of
musk and ivory

Their tiny boat is held in watery embrace
listening intently to the oceanic heart below

and the ship's churning heart below deck and their
own hearts whose valves are now

echo chambers of a command given at the
earth's inception when shadow and light

divided and sun and moon swam to their
respective orbits

and dragon seas boiled with their
incendiary breath

The captain hears all this from
time immemorial to the time when

time is no longer
and the crew's eyes become stars for

guidance in their own right
and raw sons grow to be

groves of redwood trees gazing seaward
but never leaving their watery root

and the sailors' faces look moonward
for an eternity of gently rippling waters

in a dimensionless deep space of endlessly
compassionate calm

7/5

DEATH SONNET

The shirt that one of them wore
got splattered with the other's blood

As our bodies hold in our blood
one of them is now dead

During the duel the flowing shirt
flapped dramatically in the wind

As he turned and feinted it billowed and
fell into place again and again white as snow

His head rose eagle-like out of it
as their two breaths indistinguishably panted

But in the end only one of the shirts
was splattered by the blood of the other

And as he was carried off to his mother
he realized the dead one was his brother

7/6

ONE SHOUT

One shout is all it takes
to quiet a city

One lion is all it takes
to eat a lamb

One word to smite a foe
or light a candle in a grotto

One hand to sign life's over
one eye to see the signature

A sharp blade need be no sharper
and days slide off their calendar

Dumb animals made to speak in tongues
and fish to rise in the open air

One true heart to light our lamps
and send us out to those in need

One whisper of it in perfect words
enough to tilt the planet back

to peaceful purposes

7/8

KEYHOLE

There's a keyhole in the side of a rhinoceros
and if you peek in you'll see all its

prehistory come alive

Why are there so many angels above cougars
and so seemingly few above thieves?

Where on earth did the first shirt come from
or the first pair of shoes to keep our

feet from bleeding?

(The rhinoceros is snoring in its sleep
and by its exhalations an entire rhino

alphabet in mist
is forming above its snout)

The biggest cities have their vulnerabilities
somewhere near City Hall where the

corridors of power converge

A silkily sweet blond singer is leaning back on a
highly polished black grand piano lid in a

very bright silvery spotlight

The migration over eons of four-legged and
shaggily hairy creatures has disappeared from

sight but not from hard evidence
printed on the ground

We've all been around gossip too long to be
sinlessly free of it to the point our

pure consciousness rises in a sphere of
original light to a

heaven of first causes and ultimate consequences

Lingering at the edges is all right for
children who can't swim

but not for seasoned fools like ourselves
Plunge in!

"O Christ, but the bitter sting!" etc.
as the railroad train leaves the station with

all its passenger cars in tow

Over the fence of the next hill
you can see the shimmer and the shaking

that projects this world onto our
weary screens

and if the projector's turned off and only

God's Light remains but no images or
God's blackness but no light

wouldn't instant wisdom obtain?
May we be fortunate enough to

find out
since nothing but God

goes on forever

But don't take
the easy way out

                                                                 7/10

INCENDIARY AIR

Theories abound but the toad remains
with its forelegs in Yoga position and
its back legs ready to spring

Rainbows are said to be curtains of sun-struck
prismatic droplets
and the sky's not really blue but
a reflection of the deep blue seas

We come from the saint's presence
with our saintly batteries charged to the max
and for a while the world is changed
from multiplicity to one and from
our selves to zero

They say miracles are breaks in the
natural order of things so that
waterfalls of fire say or flames of
water like the Talking Bush of Moses would be
anomalous and incidental

See through the blaze to the clearing beyond
to which all God's deer are leaping!
That's where we want to be

Near the rushing sound and the sound
stillness makes
readying for the next thing

no matter how orange its hair blazes
nor how many tails it wags as it

sails through incendiary air

7/10

TREATISE ON DISTORTION

1

"*Deliberate distortion*" says the zebra to the
tortoise just now poking its head out

"*is what the world seems made of by its
eager inhabitants*" it continues

"*and standing in front of this or that
backdrop to better – well...* stand out!" the zebra

snorts while its fellow herd-mates lower their
heads and chomp grasses while some keep a

vigilant eye peeled for the leonine breed's
slinky and sneaky connivance

closing in

2

I was about to rip the beginning of this
poem out of my notebook

but now I'm thinking I'll keep it and
populate it with as many

creatures as possible and drive everybody

wild with their yonks and gawks honks

and yowls trumpetings and grouchy growls and snorts

a deafening chorus of the present generation of
Noah's ancestry now scattered to the

four corners of the globe some in
dwindling numbers it's true and

always changing but have them sing in
trillion part harmony and they'd

raise the roof of heaven a few
notches for sure

3

Trouble is I want to start with the gnat
verifiable member of the creature community

who though not much more than an
airborne speck still we must admit

has apparent volition to go either
this way or that or even fly up our noses

or wherever it may so that as far as the
gnat is concerned it has a complete

lifetime of aversions and enjoyments
and God knows maybe even a hierarchy of

sorts with perhaps high priests and popes of the
gnat world confederacy

4

But can we say these tiny wingéd folk
are delusional or live in a

world of either make believe or out-and-out

distortion to the extent we humans do
but rather gnats live according to

God's single though multi-faceted
purpose for gnats whatever it may be that

for instance they

gather on summer porches and fly in
nattily sociable flurries in a light bulb's rays

or somehow position themselves right in our
faces as we hike forest trails hovering always

in front of our noses by some strange mechanics of
flight as if to get

a better look at these foibled humans
as we trek forward into

unknown spaces

5

And so on up the chain or out across the
sentient creaturely horizon the question of

earnestness or sincerity moot though some insects or
aquatic creatures such as the miraculous

cuttlefish use uncanny camouflage quite
cunningly to hide or surprise their

prey yet that can't really be called
I don't think either *delusion* or *distortion*

in the sense that we humans can't quite
get a true focus on the way things actually are

without somehow dying to our obfuscating
selves in a mystical sense to let their

insubstantial ashes drift to the
floor once and for all and let true

eyes (*God's Eyes*) look with pure intent and
God's own gaze at what He also

places before us with no us
left to interfere with such a

dazzling screen upon which all His
commanded shadow show dances

6

And the zebra with its zigzag stripes
melts back into the zigaggedly

striped landscape of endless zigzags
becoming almost invisible as we

might also to everyone and
all else in fact as earth-wings blow

and greater eyes than ours in their
heaven-gazed horizons

glow

7/20

DEEPMOST HEARTBEAT OF THE WORLD

> *As-tu vraiment parlé jamais à qui tu aimes?*
> — Pierre Martory

I think I'm so naked without
flesh on bones like a lightbulb

in a pile of straw lighting up a
thatched space in my zeal to

speak directly to Whom I love
(as outside I hear the red cardinal

whistle as it goes after its reflection in the
garden mirror morning after morning)

And I remain cool when my
atoms should be bursting

and seated when I should be
wildly dancing like flames as a

house burns down to its uttermost foundations

and deer scatter in the woods from fright
and trees pull back just a little of their

roots against the heat for fear of fire
and even the sun blazes a little

less to not augment the conflagration overmuch and
burn down the world

Though that's exactly what I need to do
until nothing of it or me is left

except its Arctic peaks pointing like
silver swords towards the glittering light

and its icebergs so pellucidly blue against
white and even whiter

white against yet whiter white
until nothing's left to see but a

sound so pure only His Voice could be
making it

and the
deepmost

heartbeat of the world

7/21

CONCH SHELL

What's fixed cannot be broken
what's broken cannot be fixed

Though we glue to our heart's content
and nail things together

We climb the ramparts and look out at
what or who's advancing

There's always something or someone advancing
even if it's just death

The strange world we're in and the
strange world that's inside us

Can we fix it or notice both the
falling leaves as well as their pile-up?

The strange world inside us unless it
sabotage us is gate after opening

gate into blue cloudy prairies and green
skies overturned above them

When we harness God's horses for a hard
gallop near becomes far and

far becomes near and though we may be
as lost as ever we're lost in

God's gorgeous velocity

the ruination of cities
and their ruined magistrates

as well as the curling of the
entire ocean in a conch shell

the better to hear its roars

7/22

THERE'S A SOUND

There's a buzz in the air that's not a mosquito
a honk on the street that's not a car horn

a handshake in a business deal that's
not between the businessmen

a roar of surf at the ocean that's
not the ocean's roar

There's a clamor of war that goes up
that's not from the combatants

a calling out to lost hitchhikers that
doesn't come from the search party

a crash of avalanche in the Arctic
that's not from the shattering iceberg

a wolves' howling by moonlight
that's not from the mournful wolves

There's a whisper in the ear of a lover that's
not from the weeping beloved

a crackle of fire up a stairwell
that's not from the flames

There's a noise of the world's bustle
that's not from the hustle-bustle of the world

a sigh of death from the dying
that's not from death's rattling sigh

It lifts off from the thing at hand
yet emerges from deep within it

from the passing wind that soughs through the trees
and the trees themselves creaking in the wind

but it's not from any of these
sighs or crackles creaks or love whispers

nor the grinding of the earth's rotation on its axis

nor the song of space between the planets and the
jubilant music between stars that

reaches to the outermost limits and
sings beyond them

Neither from these gazillion realities
nor from anything other than them

do these voices which are One Voice
sound and enter the

One hearing ear that is all our ears
in all our various places

nor the whirr of the oscillating fan
that swishes back and forth at

six in the morning nor the

scritch-scratch sound of my pen on the
notebook page as I write this

7/23

EON AFTER EON

A wilted flower refers to itself
in the past tense

A crossed bridge has less to look
forward to and nothing to regret

A burning building says to itself
*"If I burn to the ground we'll all be at the
same level"*

And so it goes with these grandfatherly
musings as self-conscious as a
debutante with a rip in her formal

Though no shadow falls across a
face that it doesn't caress into
greater glamour

No waterfall falls from a
great height that doesn't yell with
unbridled glee

No knock on a door by death's angel
that doesn't go unanswered though the house
become as deathly still inside to
indicate nobody's home

*(but that can continue
only so long)*

Ah the mountains wait for us to become
as wise as they

the valleys as placid and serene

the rivers as musically flowing though their

patience is never at an end and their

sanguine anticipation

eon after eon

is always kept keen

                                                7/24

SHADOWHOOD

Our shadows go only so far and then
come to an abrupt stop

If we wave our hands they wave their hands
but otherwise they have little to do with us

After hours when the sun goes down
our shadows sit in dark

bars their minds blank

One would say they are dead but they're
actually replenishing their batteries on blackness

and in the morning bright and early there they are again
extending out from us as fresh as daisies

The yearly Shadow Convention however
is truly something wonderful to behold

Special guests include shadows of the
rich and famous who may

perform or speak before the assembled
audience in perfect silence while blending in

indistinguishably with the night

By daybreak the hall is empty again with

no litter left behind and the

janitor's clack of broom or mop
and crack of daylight spread around the room

No one would imagine that hours before
the hall had been crowded from

wall to wall with our shadows
in mute attendance

each having dived within itself to the
deep source of shadowhood

Theologically speaking they are absolute
saints because absolute believers

since though they maintain their casters'
outlines they've expunged their own

selves completely and are
cast wherever they are cast

willy-nilly onto the ground at the
feet of their

Lord

APPEARANCE OF THE MUSE

The muse decided she'd present herself
fully in her natural form before her

poet so she did so with a little golden harp
in her hands and her poet

took one look past the usual beautiful
blurriness and died on the spot

So many mysteriously burnished sunsets and
fiery dawns to say nothing of

owl-hooted moonlit-thatch nights in
evocative underbrush were now

lost and dancing shadows against a
bonfire and late-night hilarious

haunted echoing in black hillsides
now had no rhapsodizer

while the *duende* knew that such a

direct appearance would kill off his
mouthpiece in a flash so he

continued to drum up the
blood with clacking heels and

shivering dark metallic reflectors from

imponderable depths bringing his
star-zonked singer to canyon edges of

unaccustomed heights and lights
with a shattering from every atom blaster

both from within and without that only
God's actual cascades of sweet solace

could both sooth and energize into
newly articulated spaces

                                                                                    7/30

THIRTY LEAN HOUNDS

Thirty lean hounds each hoarier and
more harried than the other are

pounding the tundra

Their stark and slender shadows
lunge before them but their

tongues from Hell lurch faster

from their slavering jaws

Hyenas laugh but these hellions
shatter silence with an even

greater silence in which their
taut sinews spring shapelier and

heavier than emptiness and far
holier

They'll cut through God if God not
hold them in His even swifter grip

their arching and diving front paws and
back legs churning

across wasteland more waste than land

These Hell-bound hounds with their
laser-beam eyes ahead of them

heading for alienation

— *Let them!*

7/31

WHITMAN

While my wife was massaging my sore
right arm in bed I suddenly

saw the Civil War soldiers in the
hospital Whitman used to visit

and how they didn't know who he
was or who he would be or

that he'd written *Leaves of Grass*

but only that he wrote letters home for them
and wiped their brows with cold cloths or

leaned close to them to hear their
whispered words and leaned close with his

sky blue eyes and pink face to
kiss their beards

and gaze long at them and
hold their hands while they

died

8/3

LITTLE DOOR IN THE HEART

A little door in the heart opens
and floods the earth in its streaming

golden rays both inwardly and outwardly
gilding boat masts at harbor in Madagascar

as they clang against piers
or down shafts of diamond mines

illumining the cheekbones and eye sockets of
South African miners as they descend

and this light also enables a few
miles more inward on that more

silent journey that takes place whether or
not we notice toward eternal arctic weather

and ribboning interplanetary breezes
where the milestones have been placed

by previous trudgers and flyers whose
names also gild our lips with a

more comprehensive remembrance
into whose expanded domain God's own

Light slants in as if a
larger door in our hearts opens

not by our labors alone but by
the focus of our deepest celebration and His

most Merciful Attendance

China could not be more near
nor albatross flight more easeful

across sky so blue it
puts eyes in its pellucid clarity

above oceans so still and green
they seem more like valleys than seas

on earth more benign than terrible
in a curved Universe that surrounds us

on all sides
with song

8/4

IF OUR DAYS ARE NUMBERED

If our days are numbered
I wonder what number day this is

The Zurich pre-dawn is so still
yet I hear cars on a distant road

The world is so still
yet like pins in a pin cushion

you can hear screams

It's all creakings and chill breezes
and a sound like a waterfall

that isn't a waterfall

Posture is important they say
as our skeletons try to make sense of the days

I dreamt I was going to be taught the piano
but woke up before the first lesson

I thought as I sat up I could
put a grand piano in our small living room

over my wife's objections

A church has struck the quarter hour
as I wait the 4 a.m. dawn prayer

and the cats are restless

Are our numbers on our foreheads
or in the lines of our hands?

Are there beams from the stars
with our numbers on them?

Saying God knows the numbers of our days
previous to their fulfillment

and that they were cast within us at birth

and that with us their dice rolls in
the universe with rounded edges

calculating every move we make
toward our mortality

until the zero rings like a
sudden snowfall of hidden light

seeing the deer bound away from us
in silver herds up the

sides of precarious mountains
and water draw back to its source

and the air go out of the shimmering
sails that have gotten us here

to this particular point pinpointed at

this particular spot on our

earthly trajectory in our suddenly
halted progression toward

living forever

so that instantaneously God's Face
looks in at every window at once

and where we usually look out through our
eyes He now looks in

and every portal in this sphere is
filled with angelic inhalations

is to give silence itself an elemental
presence and precedence over the

noise of the world
even as at this moment on a

balcony in Switzerland at 4 a.m.
there's only the soft ringing in my

usual ears and waves upon waves of
soft sound in the distance

like a waterfall that isn't a waterfall
in an air that is air in an overcast sky

obscuring the innumerable stars

8/5

SEEKING AND FINDING

The true seeker hasn't gone anywhere nor
seen anything but Allah

The true finder hasn't discovered but
what Allah has had him or her find in

all his or her seeking

Nor lost but what Allah has exchanged
Himself for in all his or her

seeking and finding

And everything is already

right where you're

sitting

8/6

LUCERNE STREET AT NIGHT

Lucerne Street at night with tour buses parked
(very European ones with huge front windows)

Bicyclists whizzing by and Vespas and
very small cars zooming past all sounding like

sewing machines
Amber lights in the street lamps

Passing babies cry in Swiss passing dogs
bark in dog this warm summer night

with taxis careening around corners

and streets going off at angles more
back alleys than streets

and all the motors sound different than
in America here everything whispering

Then two guys saunter by speaking
Swiss German I can't understand

though they're saying very normal things in
natural voices

about just about anything or
nothing of much importance though of

value in the cosmic scheme of things
that could change lives by even so

much as a gnat's wing from one
extreme to another and suddenly and

definitively lift one of us or all of us
into cylindrical rotations of

indelible starlight

8/6

THE HEAVENLY DOOR THAT IS ALWAYS OPEN

The heavenly door that is always open
is oiled to the point its hinges ring in

High C by our remembrance and our
relaxing into God's better handling of

all our affairs

We look into a cave and see shadows
We peer into a tunnel hoping to see

our exit under a starry night or sun-
drenched day

when the entire universe turned
inside-out is already within us I

say sitting in a little hotel bathroom at
2:45 a.m. to not wake my sleeping wife

and the world asleep or awake outside
not particularly waiting for this news

as squid slide by long-tentacled through the
deeps and stags on hilltops in

rust silhouette stand out against the
sunset stock still before bounding away

There's no end to the excitement of these
proclamations even if one gnat swerve by them

out of a line of death-dealing spray or a single
sparrow fly off with its least crumbs from the

glistening tiny white table on the terrace where we
last ate tea and cake and none of these

thoughts had yet occurred to me

Supreme light is everywhere available past our
senses to that sensation of the infinite that so

ennobles and assails us in our
endless waking dreams

The song of it leaps from our throats our mouths
opened or closed to decorate the

undersides of the celestial boat with our
idiosyncratic constellations

Let me never tire *O God* of Your
inspiration though my head be drowsy with the

low wine of this world's dregs

Let if only one leaf of Your High Tree fall onto
my tongue my heart leap at the

chance to animate its disintegration into
a radiant biological skeleton of

vein framework where once Your

leafy handiwork stood so
elementally green in Your original

atmosphere before
entering the heart's conundrum

8/10

Hotel Rigi, Weggis, Switzerland
(attending son's wedding)

THIS PLANE'S FULL OF BABIES

This plane's full of babies

so it's a jet propelled by gurgles and
bubbling coos vocal and gestural

experiments forward from Zurich to Paris
on a blue sunny morning

where these future generations long after
we've disembarked from this planet

will carry on blithely without us
flying in personal planes or individual

rocket packs from place to place

while we hopefully and peacefully
circulate among the greater stars

8/11

AS WE FLY FORWARD

As we fly forward we're going
backwards in time

within limits

Not as in a Jean Cocteau movie
we won't land in wigs and velvet coats with
buttons down the front riding carriages

though I had a strange sensation as we
fly in our Air France Air Bus back home
watching horses gallop as this huge plane
groans through the sky

of the
simultaneity of transport at full
forward lurch

arriving where? At full gallop or
jets awhirr pushing air through them
to propel us

into territories we've never
visited before?

Is the home we're going back to the
same home we left?

Eleven days is an earthquake or avalanche

between life and death
The whole earth opens to its molten core
in eleven days

The entire heavens finally wrap around their
own ends and loop inward or outward at last
in eleven days

A new whale is born from its mammalian mother's
womb in eleven days to add to the pod in deep
twinkling waters

The king is dead and the rabble have set up a
guillotine for the nobles in eleven days

We could step off the plane at our destination
in the Cambrian period (*forget Cocteau!*)

or the Pleistocene with its horny creatures

or suddenly be sitting at God's pristine table
with golden and ruby fruits set out for our
original tasting

each atom of our being renewed

And shoot forward back to this plane again
in the vividly humdrum reality of our
passage and metallic mode of travel

no more wise than before

though nourished from hidden springs
in the instant of our motion

above the Atlantic Ocean

8/11

PARADISE GATE

In Memoriam Mahmoud Darwish

The exile dies and
finds he goes home

All lamented fig trees and
cups of pungent coffee steam in the air at once

All horses tied to trees
lonely without their donkeys in green pastures

All glimpses of the ocean from afar
across the barbed wire of enemy territory

held in a vibrant wisp in the
air for a split second before dispersal

at lickety-split speed over the earth's mirror
as the world spins its cloudy top below

And a grieving exile opens his eyes
now polished to a precious sapphire sheen

on unforeseen landscapes not exactly
reassembled from the nostalgic gazes in his

poems but partaking of certain
mosaic resemblances jigsaw-puzzled together

and he also sees Paradise Gate open before him
— and his living doubts and denials

now banished as brutally as he was
to inconsequential territories —

floating under fig trees
wrapped in fresh roasted

aromas of coffee
at home at last

among his equally
departed comrades

8/13

BREAD WAS BUTTER AND BUTTER BREAD

Bread was butter and
butter bread

A telephone rang
with a wooden clack

A door was ice
hot to the touch

Cattle meowed as a
black sun rose

Flame simmered down
around a round white egg

Our faces appeared
in the air

in God's ear

8/13

THE DOCTOR'S ARRIVED

The doctor's arrived on the back of a horse
a star wedged deep in his bag

by which I mean not a sheriff's badge but a celestial body
streaming through space at enormous velocities

"*OK stick out your tongue let's hear your heart
percuss your kneecaps look in your ears*

*Can you see three fingers or four or five?
Can you make out the distant hills on fire?*"

His black coat flags in the wind like a sail
and gravity doesn't seem to anchor him down

I see past his moonlike face past the trees
to hills in the distance burning like suns

Even the sky's bronze now and he looks in my eyes
and I'm vaporized as quick as they try to blink closed

Even the usual unstable rumbling has increased
and what once seemed firm is turning in circles

Windows cloud over with what looks like bird flight
Floors become rolling green sea waves in sunlight

His voice directs movements I never experienced
my feet treading matter as if it were water

He's got me from inside yet nothing's been opened
I'm turned inside out by the deftest of touches

Earth and all its inhabitants are angels
earth air and water have all become fire

Not the fire of burning but of pure transformation
so what's earth becomes gold and what's

gold becomes diamond

He pulls out a star from the depths of his bag
and tosses it through me to the height of the sky

and I'm suddenly cured of what I didn't know
was killing me

Shriven and naked as glass
through which nothing is glimpsed

8/15

STOPS

The play goes on for a few hours
then stops

The players may go on many hours more
then stop

Finally even stop stops
and we're in eternity

which having never started
never stops

though this poem and its poet
stop

unless we're already
in eternity

full stop

8/20

ORPHEUS AT REST

A head comes to a stop after
rolling down a hill

and begins speaking to the
grasshoppers and dragonflies

We have to bend quite close to it to
hear it for it speaks in a low whisper

Where has it been to have been so
cruelly severed?

What did it do or say that it should
come to this so far from its body?

What advice does it have for those
creatures in the grass or hovering just

above the grass whirring iridescent wings?

Why can't we keep our heads or
why can't we lose them in the right

way and for the right reasons?
Leave off headiness for love's portions?

Or have them settle in for once
and show a bit of seasoned mahogany sheen

a bit of true wisdom and heartfelt eloquence?

The grasshopper listens for a moment
then hops away

The dragonfly hovers then speeds off

The lips keep whispering to perhaps just
the surrounding air or the trillion blades of grass

Orpheus so far from his true music

Even the trees bashful in his presence
throwing shade across his

last and perfect silence

8/21

THE DESPERADOS

Desperados from the time of Jesse James
ride into town but it's already been plundered

Nothing of this world of any intrinsic worth
is left in the coffers safeboxes or banks

I mean it's all still there as crisp as ever
but as worthless as dust in the ultimate accounting

Gold so malleable so beautiful so yellow
shining like suns to drive sane men mad

Having already stolen some of their glory from the sun
even these glitterings've become dull and flat

The treasure behind the treasure and the
worth inside the worth stay as

intact as if they were safeguarded by an
army of jinn

The treasure worth looting that comes at the
heart's radiant bidding is as

luscious as ever as if enveloped in skin
like pomegranate seeds in their hard shelled fortresses

The whole world's this way
with its enticing façades

that the camera keeps grinding to make it
all look so real

the mental lens inside us that lends
reality to flimsiness

polishing worth out of
worthlessness

Heartbreaking thunderous static lightning-flashes of
illumination in strands of

infinite pearls and the diamonds of eternity
held up in the hands of the truly

poor in God's sight who own everything
who in their utter worthlessness in this

world have become
this world's kings

The desperados drink and still die
of thirst

Gamble and their own soul's
chips fly away

Pillage and rampage and it's
they who get trampled

Only One sees the treasure behind the treasure

and worth in the worthless and the
golden sun in total darkness

When we swim up in that light
The town is ours

though we've become nothing

We see its true Owner
and love beheads us at last

We're purged and made populous
at one stroke of luck

Tattered and crowned in one
shattering instant

as the sad desperados
ride out totally bereft

8/24

BEGINNINGS AND ENDINGS

As soon as one story ends another
begins in this world

As soon as one story begins
another ends

The ship entering the harbor in thick
fog loaded with explosives may be

the end or beginning of a story but is
rarely the middle or else in fact

all stories begin in the middle and there really
are neither ends nor beginnings but only

a single interrupted continuum in kinds of
scenario hiccups that seem pristine unto

themselves and that ship just now
sliding into the dock with its ghostly

crew and mad captain is in the
middle of its own destiny to explode or

not and cause irreparable havoc on this
night of all nights when the Pleiades are so

vivid above the fog and there seems to be
a divine shadow bending over the

cosmos irradiating every revolving entity with
both terrestrial and extraterrestrial love

and though darkness may either
descend from seemingly above or

ascend from seemingly inside us to
make our actions insidious in the world rather than

amative or frankly amorous

still the middle of the story extending out at
both sides is one of endless illumination

with more depth and breadth of meaning than the
hot flashing blast from that

ship as it suddenly blows itself
sky high to fling scattered

fragments among the stars

8/26

OLD MAN IN A DROP OF WATER

There's an old man in a drop of
water whose lips break the

surface enough to articulate delight

He tumbles inside it like a Chinese gymnast
rolling always forward and

curling up in almost embryo fashion

In other drops there's an old woman
whose white hair floats behind her

and whose eyes peer out in glittering wonder

How many drops in the world at
any one time and so how many

old men of wisdom and women of light

keeping the stories alive between them
as they flow in a cascade or

out of a faucet to wash our hands
or splash water on our faces after sleep?

Their murmur keeps the world happy
in spite of its intrinsic darkness

These drops of water singing to us and
spying wide-eyed at the sheer

miracle of our existence

8/27

DIVINE NAME

God

I've tossed Your Name around like candy
and made it bay at the moon

like the howling of wolves
on a cold midnight

I've said it with a
temple reverberation as if in

prehistoric space

or a black cloud gathering strength
above a boiling sea

hiding its most precious treasures
in its briniest deeps

I've thrown it around God
in loose neighborhoods and

tight soirées

against windows as if unrolling
revolutionary banners to an

unbelieving populace below

or expressing its articulate enunciation
as if it were gossamer webs on

Himalayan crags

Whispered it to my own soul
as if it were a family of mouse dignitaries

inside the wainscoting of my
swift mortality

and wandered into the
forest of its true sound with only a

small net and dim flashlight
already flickering

Until Your Name bursts from our lips
the way creation first burst from Your utterance to *"Be!"*

should we all be like
graves on a hillside

basking in the sun?

Or an energetic twist in the sky in
outer space waiting for a

cosmic event to appear?

Flexibility of tongue

Ease of heart

Intensity of eye

Silence above all
in Your deepest chambers

God of no Name
Your Name stands for

Heart-hold with no
floor beneath us

in our dire poverty?

9/1

UNTIL COCKCROW WAKE US

Where is that one gone who
showed me the way?

The yard is full of roosters
their red combs flopping over

The air is full of their indistinguishable gurglings
and the ground's been crossed and

recrossed so often no clear trail
shows in the dirt

How did I get here
so far from any source of

human satisfaction?

Can I wait for the stars to come out
to aid my navigation?

Like everything else
the sky's so far away

and the other wanderers
so inhospitable

The fact that we're here at all
should be enough!

The trees that line the perimeters
so full of singing birds

They're not complaining
all day tied to a search for food

I'm at least free to
dance and wave my arms

Dance and stamp my
own tracks in the dust

crisscrossed by boot prints tire tracks
and billions of chicken feet

as innumerable as stars

A feeling of raw desolation's
invaded my soul

I could cry out God's Name
but fear its hollow echo among the

slanted shacks and empty vehicles
abandoned everywhere

as the dust we all become
arises to cover us

and the voice we are
gets fainter and fainter

Abdal-Hayy's among them,
until cockcrow wake us

9/3

THE THRESHOLD OF THE FLOOR

The threshold of the floor is
low enough to reach

but unlimited Presence is
what I seek

How can that be when I
do things in hiding

knowing You are everywhere and
Aware yet vainly

veiling myself from Your Face which
goes naked from

time before time so that
I am the veiled one!

There's only one recourse for me
beside staying among wild creatures

my own harsh animal among them
climbing trees that will

always shake me down

Take off all secrecy from the
nakedness of my being

and let Your Light flood every
corner that now seeps everywhere

already

except to my blind ocular tubes
hiding behind black glasses

What's the use of yearning for
what I refuse to set out for

reviling the unveiled moment
whose presence is already present?

A stone among stones
along the unpaved road

A knobless door I only need
put a knob on

A prayer to You
I only need believe in

A soreness in the dark
only You can soothe

9/3

THE OYSTER IS IN DEEP MEDITATION

The oyster is in deep meditation
turning a speck of irritation

into a pearl

The devastating forest fire is
anxiously pursuing its destiny to find

both its source and its ultimate
legacy

The sky serenely continues to be
above it all

an enviable latitude for those of
us below

Grinding gears in the most
complex machinery are meshed in a

battle of both their iron wills and well-oiled
cooperation

Push the curtain aside in all this
onto the empty chamber reverberating endlessly

with God's nuclear light

Come in under a raindrop as big as

Saturn and find the Originator of

raindrops bigger than the Name
that is greater than

all the entire universes combined

and smaller than that which
pushes our heartbeats into a

greater glory than any of us could know
by ourselves alone

as each ant goes to its task
as certain of its purpose as any

dust mote falling precisely into place
through space on both the tippy-top of

Kilimanjaro and
our dusty nearly vanishing selves here in the

deep earth crater that most suits us
and gives us comfort

9/6

BLIND SAMSON

Blind Samson ran around the building three times
yet concealed his true strength in his

fists before God impelled him to use it

at which point no temple however
tall and pillared under a clear

blue sky filled with crossing birds
could withstand the extra-dimensional

strength of his human muscles
the way a volcano lies dormant under

grassy hillsides with munching cows
until God by an earthly heaving deep inside

the sleep of mortality suddenly
looses its strength and Pompeii

becomes deathly silent and sulfurous

Fumes instead of fluffy clouds
hang over the pleasure gardens

where phallic statues lie
buried

and ignoble rubble stretches
for miles

9/8

LOVE'S UP CLOSE AND PERSONAL CONFLAGRATION

Unemployed angels watch the visions all day
of mortals who are about to die

Others are specialists in rescue at sea
salvaging living souls from lifeboats or those

desperately clinging to wreckage

Others are last-minute angels
catching (when things are about to

really go off the rails) their victims
with deft grasp

and after holding them close to
their own snow-beating hearts putting them

gently down again safe and sound

as the freight train screams past or the
earth simply appears again

under their feet

These spirits are vigilant wide awake and
atomically everywhere

in all sizes and somehow placed in that

onion-thin shield between life and death

(though of course they flow freely between each
and have no preference for either)

But their sudden appearance actively
in otherwise static or inert circumstances

gives them acrobatic advantages to pluck
some of us out of trees or out of

harm's way shifting an inevitability
from certainty to a sweet ambiguity

as only the angelic can
which for us saves the day completely

from certain though undestined annihilation

They are here with us as well when we
go forward into pitch blackness

one spotlit step at a time to the
Noblest Encounter when sudden

light is switched on in even the
thickest forest and grace is seen

visibly falling in bright flakes
through the trees

There's nowhere they aren't and
everywhere they are at all times

doing God's good bidding
and our imperfect indwelling

and their mysterious names
are silently repeated

on the lips of our heartbeats from
birth onwards the way

arched doors in a majestic building lead
in to the radiant chamber at the

center where the King resides

whose face projects through all their
angelic faces at once and sparks fly into

place out of every atmosphere
to form love's up close and personal

conflagration

9/15

SO MANY THINGS TO SAY

There are so many things to say
and only one mouth and one heart

to say them with

Sailboats on the high seas
filled with Tahitians

Venetian blinds in a shadowy
European town around noon

Monsoon winds and screaming rains
battering tin roofs to staccato rattling

Gloom and doom on the composer's
mind as he struggles at the piano

to find just the right notes to say it
and avoid all the wrong

The gong on Mount Kailash struck
once by a hooded monk and its

resounding song going on long across the
deep valley

and yet these are all just
one thing said

before I go to bed

9/19

NOTHING TO DO

There was a star-crossed lover
only the star was crossing inside

the heaven of his head
and it joined a choiring constellation of

equally amiable astros all in
crystalline formations seen not from

this side as mythical figures from Greece
but from the other side as

pure illuminations whose rays reach every
single soul of us in incessant celebration

He gazed with his beloved eyes at the
Beatrice-like beloved of the skies

his head having dissolved into
stratospheric dimensions so that excessively

distant lights in the night sky were now
lamps for him to read by

The sails of sailboats point upward
while their rudders lean down into

depths

He saw as if through a straw
into outermost space

Nothing contains Him
and He contains the

nothing that is
as well as the

nothing that isn't

to a celestial music

This love couldn't stumble into a
delicatessen and ask for pig's trotters

Nor proclaim the pinwheel revelations of his inside skies
on any street corner but the corner on

Secret Street

in a city only few know although
all of us wander through

wondering what to do

When there's nothing in either world
except God's Light

to do

9/20

WE DO THINGS

We do things
but who's the doer?

The wind blows
but who's the blower?

A lark sings
but who's the singer?

A bell rings
our ears ring

and awaken

but whose ears are
ringing when the

bell rings?

Whose hearts are
shaken?

9/22

ONE QUICK COLD NIGHT

One quick cold night is all it takes
for leaves to snap and

fall from trees

Greensward now more
goldsward with yellow and brown

mosaics underfoot

I love really old black and white
silent movies and Wagner operas

that make us think of primordial
beginnings so lost in the fogs of

the past there's only vestiges left and
mythological excesses

Did Jason and the Argonauts make the
voyage or thousands of merchants

sailing for gold now boiled
down to one

representational hero?

Green lush summer in one night
turns to fall

soon tree boughs will be bare
and you can see through the

forest to surrounding city streets
though at the height of summer

it's as dense and thick as
any first forest on earth

with or without good and evil
elves living in it with

acorn cap hats and squirrel-carriage steeds

All journeys are metaphorical after all
to the single real journey no metaphor

can adequately capture

though we wear its soul's tattoos in our
flesh forever and as we

slide or stumble from state to state or
station to station we get

gradually transformed into gold

and though our leaves fall onto the
forest floor what branches remain

are brilliant and bare

SYNOPSIS OF A NONEXISTENT TRILOGY

1

We learn in the first book an
explorer with a long Latin name

lands feet first on an island populated
by creatures half man half elephant

who eat the luscious heart-shaped fruits
that grow by the water

and whose government structure is
one based on size and age only

so that the oldest and biggest
are lorded over by the youngest and smallest

thus leaving the oldest freedom to
browse and ruminate to their

hearts' content to the end of their
days

2

In the second book the
matter at hand is the

origin of matter and the
origin of the great river that

flows through the continent bringing great
fertility some years and other years

drought

Expeditions are organized of which our
hero as intrepid as he is heroic

trains thousands of natives by
speaking their native tongue with the

eloquence of their mythic first man
out of whose tongue tumbled their own

language fully formed and blazing with
highly polished beauty they've

tried for millenniums to approximate
(their belief that every spoken

statement is trying to find that
first perfection and always

falls short so that even their
poet shamans enter trances

to reconnect to that pure eloquence
but always come out weeping)

3

By the third book we're thrown into a
labyrinth of possibilities as

complex as the mosaics on a
Moroccan mosque wall into whose

stratosphere of patternings the mind and
heart of us spin to a stasis then to an

ecstasis
out of which fly radiant plumaged birds

One gate falls and another rises

One rose garden appears and the
gushing pond in its center swallows

us and garden in a single gulp and we
find ourselves at an outer edge seeing

our galaxy from a cross-section slice as
thin as breath

Windows open onto windows and floating
phrases interlink as separate

corpuscles in the floating body of our lives

that single biological entity entering

wisdom in its meridians and heartbeats

each engraving the very book we're
reading in the very process of our

reading it

                                                                               10/9

A SMATTERING OF CONUNDRUMS

It's an itch that won't get scratched
a nod that won't get nodded

An ardor that won't get awarded
an odor that won't get added

A do that won't get done
a done that won't get undone

An answer that won't get answered
a ran that won't get run

O mountain of mountains whose
measure is man

don't topple on us
to unspin our span

                                                                10/12

NOWHERE WAS EMPTINESS UNRIVERED

He sat in a river that flowed
over his head

in the heat of the day
at midnight

Nothing perturbed the
flow of his thoughts

which came to a halt
at a golden door

into which streamed sheep
from the mountainside

their flanks aquiver

The sun shone down
and the stars poured in

to his heart's red valley
as it pounded

and all the lights in the
heavens opened their

spectacular ventricles
replacing him

His face reflected the
starry radiance

His toes quivered
as the sheep entered

Nowhere was emptiness
unrivered

Nor the river of emptiness
levered

Nor his soul from its Source
severed

10/15

LIVING FLAME

It's a piece of flesh with
eyeholes we look out of

heart pounding
mind racing

on skates across an icy lake
whose trees reflect in the slick glass

or standing still or
horizontally asleep

chamois around a living fist
skin sail blown by an

inner wind

locating ourselves
where we are

an apex of cross-hairs
in whose moving sight

we move
never out of range

blown by an updraft
through time

heart pounding
on an unclosed door

mind racing
in divinity's circle

a breath away
from our source and end

hands up in
supplication

gray light
turning rainbow

Through these eyes we see
neither where we've been

nor where we're going
but only Him in invisibly

naked glory

each notch of the way
accompanied by

bones

Lord of us all
O Living Flame!

10/15

IF I HAD TO SAY AT THIS MOMENT

If I had to say at this
moment what it's all

about
the final word

in my room at night
throb-sound of a distant clock

space like an
arch of the night above me

alone at the side of my bed
the house around me on earth

my wife asleep on the
top floor and the

cat asleep on a
chair somewhere unseen

by me
all of us in our own selves

alive to it awake or
sleeping

a white noise hum in my head
and tentative pauses in the

writing
waiting

being seen rather than
seeing though not by me

clearly

and keep at bay the
roasted landscapes

the hard-as-nail part
the mallet-strike

What it's all about

a white wall in a
white altitude

a splendor in
simplicity

ever the silent music
ever more silent

tuning up

unpaused continuum

nothing behind nor
before

our original
solitude

praises and
wakings

10/18

BLINDLY BELIEVING

Of the depth of the treasure to be
dug I was never certain

but of the location below the
X on the map I was always dead sure

Though the map had come to me casually
I implicitly trusted the source of it

even if its transmitter had
betrayed me on another occasion

Once the map itself was in my
hands and supple to my constant

rolling and unrolling as if now
custom-tailored to its new owner

it had taken on an almost divine
absoluteness of its own and I never

doubted its veracity and looked to it
as both authority and guide

It was now simply a question of
excavation of digging on occasions of

inspiration from the unriddling of a
few words or a few opening lines

come to me on nonconspiratorial air
when no one else was looking nor

even in the slightest concerned
leaving me to my own devices

and I generally worked at night
by a small but intense

radiance enough to show me the
depth to go and to light up

a considerable area of dimensionless space

For shovel and pick I relied
on my own ingenuity and for their

practical and most expedient
shapes I relied on what my good

Lord would supply in a blueprint of
vision somehow both pristinely

new and somehow going back to the
very first excavators who ever

had in their hearts on this hard
earth that there was

treasure to be had

God knows we were raw and unequipped and
rash in our forwardness on the

project though dedicated from the
very secret cores of us

and the heavens if anything seemed to
lean in our favor

for the first pick-strikes bore sparks
and the first shovelfuls bore

headway on depth even if only a
worm's length though that

worm be our own mortality

I never doubted the project nor its
outcome ultimately for as I dug so

treasure was revealed even before the
final wealth sought could be

obtained
in sunny days or sour overcast or

pure

O treasure beyond price
hammered by the constant

heartbeats of our souls!

CODA

Invisible God
reveal to me Your plan

but let me continue to dig
for Your sake

blindly believing

10/20

OPTICAL ILLUSIONS

Optical illusions abound in the optical field
aural illusions abound in the

sound realm

That waterfall you hear is just
someone walking toward you

That wall rising up and that sky falling down is
just your own eyelids closing

seen
from inside

The world evaporates and reappears
inside a fish tank

entwined in goldfish grass

Our loved ones also undergo illusory
transformations

sometimes as fleet horses leaping turnstiles in
synchronized equine unison

other times as lone silhouettes in a white
paper moonlight sitting under a gnarly

black tree

Our own souls color what we see
and what we see when we see

is our own souls

To get out of the way to see what
God sees isn't for every ant and gorgon to

accomplish in one lifetime but it's a
commendable goal

and worth every once of our
strength

That window opening onto that
snow crystal hillside with the

slanted birches on it rising
all the way into heaven

That white rabbit there between them
leaving whiteness and

entering it again

even whiter than
before

10/21

GEESE OVERHEAD

When there's a change and
something's gone

something new has a way of
slithering into its place

both blending in somehow with
its environment as if it weren't

at all in the old pattern's emptiness
as well as celebrating with a subtle

fireworks with buttered popcorn and
distant piano music

leaving us *(while still grieving in
some ways over the recent loss even if

the change was for the better)* somewhat
dumbfounded at the swift

transformation

the way leaves cover over where a
rock's plopped in

and even the sound of the plop now
echoing in our memory

alone at the side of a pond
marveling at the honking of

geese overhead

10/24

THE PRACTICE OF POETRY

The practice of poetry is an
ivory dog keeping silver sheep

in their proper pasture
though all are alive with no trace of
either ivory or silver but a

strange kind of flesh and blood that
glows in the dark and

dazzles in daylight

Poetry's what we hum to ourselves as we
wind down the tower stairs or in
more hectic moments

cry out as we spiral upward

each shout igniting a new star in an
infinite firmament

while also all the while simply
wriggling slightly under our pen tip

in a wan electric light with the
writing hand itself casting a

shadow on the page

And yet at the very top of the
mountain in both high

headwinds and strong snow-sheets it's what
message we pass from sherpa to sherpa in

short expressive bursts both to
keep from freezing altogether as well as
keep our hopes up that we'll descend
safely with astonishingly extravagant
bright blue vistas etched forever in our hearts

though no one may be waiting to
hear them when we're down below again

among men

The practice of poetry is also the
volcano's red glow against the

night and then a few days later
the plume and finally the

flow that comes like hot tears down
all inclines to cover ancient
villages with both

death and preservation

It's God's calling when He calls
and our mutability in both

mute speech and talkative silence

and sometimes song that threads itself with
flittering chickadees in the trees

It's a cold soul turned against the
mirror to become warm

and a locomotive bearing down on its
victim who gratefully gets out of the

way just in time and goes on to lead a
far better life

I've counted the threads in
poetry's carpet that

flies and stays grounded
sometimes simultaneously

though this one's enough for us in the
shade of this tree under a

table set for tea

and its intricate weave that
continues along the earth

mingling sweetly among its grasses
whose green blades are now indistinguishable

from the carpet's threads in day's

metrically
unraveling light

                                                      10/29

I LIE FACE DOWN

I lie face down on my bed
feeling the warm ship's hull of my

heartbeats

10/29

TO THE ONENESS

A lone oriole sings to the Oneness of God
The throne of a king sings to the Oneness of God

Each oak as a model oak perfect in
every way sings to His Oneness

A tattered cloak on a pole in a high wind
sings to His Oneness

A single cry in the night nearby
sings to His Oneness

The entirety of the circling cosmos
sings to His Oneness

Each of us seven billion persons on earth
in our single centrality

while the trillion river flows
sings to His Oneness

Each one a cosmos singing that Oneness
just as every single night cricket

out of all the possible crickets
sings to His Oneness

And while things that fall fall singly
and make their own particular falling noise as they fall

just as buildings under demolition fall inside their
own latitudes in clouds of dust

so a single hammer blow sings
to the Oneness of God

and the scarlet flash of a single parrot flying
in a jungle canyon

sings magnificently to God's Oneness

and that everything perishes constantly before that
single Face of God that remains imperishably

past all cosmic dust clouds circling silently
or grinding in orbits as they go each

orbit of which in its solitudinous round
sings to God's Oneness

and the rest of this song sings to His Oneness
all bits left out and all inspiration exhausted

after it's gone and only the
singing remains and even that finally

extinguished

So even that silence
never completely silent

sings to His Oneness

TO GET TO SLEEP

To get to sleep lately I've gotten into bed
on my back and first faced
left for a time for my body to

stretch and get used to being horizontal
then after a time I roll over and
with hands under pillow to support my
head face right which was the

sunnah also of the Prophet Muhammad peace be
upon him and preferred among us though I
confess that to get to sleep if really
restless I'll go onto my stomach with

head facing to my left which in the
bed is then the right and kind of

roll over from left to right until the
burrowing is complete and I
sink into sleep

I wonder how others do it?
George Washington with his wig off

how he got himself to sleep to be the
fairly rested father of our country or

Napoleon if he had to
tuck his hand over his belly first before

managing to snooze or if poor

Joan of Arc had to sleep in her
chain mail just anywhere in a
manger perhaps with its
evocative overtones and whether she
could just lie down exhausted and be
fast asleep or if she had her angels
lull her softly into it

What did Salvador Dali do
Did he have to be between two white
horses facing in opposite directions and
holding ripe cucumbers over his
chest the way the pharaohs do those little
golden sheep crooks?

Did Mozart just curl up to sleep?
Falling into Costanza's embrace? Tunes in his
head?

Bach straight as a board on his back
staring up at the baroque ceiling with its pure
mathematical proportions until a kind of
hypnosis came over him?

And did the first cave people kind of
huddle together like bears in their
furs as if in hibernation some turned
one way some turned another?

I can't imagine Einstein asleep except in a
big overstuffed chair having finally
run his poor brain into the ground
or out into space and just conked
out with head on an armrest perhaps
his pipe safely stowed in an ashtray by
his side

All the multitudes in their
sleep-getting attitudes and
variations

and looking at the weird lank contortions our
cat gets into I won't even attempt to
imagine the rest of the natural world with its
tree sloths and pangolins

And now that I've written this my
continued bedtime experimentations each time as if
for the first time will be conducted
again until I somehow miraculously

doze off for some hopefully
well-earned rest
after making this hopefully at least small

contribution to humanity's relaxation

into the sweet deep darkness of sleep

11/2

SILENT STONES

Silent stones break their silence
and break their stoniness

Lions' manes remain and
maintain their leonine maniness

Trees everywhere evergreen or
less evergreen evade summer's greeniness

in a world most itself when it
sheds itself in fall's unselfishness

And we in our wearily worldly wisdom
weave no weapons but welcome

                                                                                     11/5

SOME JUGGLER!

Some juggler! He comes on
stage and juggles his own bones!

Bicycle wheels in the air that slide
sideways in space then disappear

"Heads will roll" they say
but he simply juggles them

I've seen him look at trees in the forest in a
way you know he'd like to

hoist them aloft and make them spin
but they remain hunkered down

their roots well gripped

You meet him halfway or even all the way
and get a giddy feeling he'd like to

hurl you up with some of your
friends or family and keep you all

rotating happily in midair for as
long as it takes

to change your ways

He juggles where and nowhere with the
same cool aplomb until this world loses its

weight altogether and gets those
fuzzy edges things get whirring in space

Yet nothing's ever lost
it's all here

lovingly held in
love's atmosphere

11/10

ENTER THE CLOWNS

Enter the clowns and we discover
they're the most serious of all

and the serious ones the most laughable
or at least the most flawed

These idiots flop through hoops leap through
flames and screech at nothingness

smiling and surprised as if the world full of
dangers were a simpleton's game

while the serious ones watching them hurriedly
cavort because there's no tomorrow

sit increasingly in their own incoherence
watching more and more through their

own rational chaos and mayhem

to the distant sounds of
roaring lions

11/11

THE SMELL OF WET SACKCLOTH

The smell of wet sackcloth and tallow
permeates the monk's cell

The smell of wet grass and fresh blood
permeates the tiger's den

The smell of tiny little fresh afterbirth of babies
permeates the mouse warren

Across the canyon floats the smell of
morning fog and pine

In a downtown Manhattan office building
the smell of ammonia and air freshener

Fresh asphalt gives off its own smell
and roofs being tarred can be

detected all the way down the block

Follow a scent to its source and you
may be in Samarkand or the nearby fruit market

Toledo Ohio or Cathay on the spice route
the tiniest indication by a subtle detail

to the whole that awaits us not in
the dragon's coiled tail in his

grotto reeking of recently eaten knights
(their armor discarded like oyster shells)

but in the overwhelming olfactory radiance of
perfection in which our odorous

imperfections dissolve

and when we reach the valley
an intermingling of hollyhocks and

fresh mown hay might overtake us

or else a sudden disappearance of all
scents but heaven-sent ones

in which our own thickset sensorium
is absorbed

in the weave of their
weightless breeze

11/14

A SHOUT UNHEARD

In Memoriam Marco Antonio Montes de Oca

A shout unheard
A cry behind the latticework

A sunny day turned to night in an instant
stars shooting sparks like shorted light bulbs

where we're suddenly forced to navigate
by our own light

Walls going up at random between us
and between us and the sea and sky

Whimpering in a matchbox
Sobbing in the barrel of a gun

No one holds all the cards
but our facial expressions tell all

as the last bridge explodes
and fish below swim serenely on

11/20

IN ALL ORACULAR SONG

In all oracular song
some short some long

I see events in a distant glade
brought nearer

Though none may see the Unseen
its immaculate detectables are there

for all to see
and here in a glittery globe

to be detected

Something for everyone
means just that

No soul goes unnourished
on this score

Though at sea in a boat the
size of a teacup

and a wave the size of a house
overtake us

and the ship go down with all hands
and all handles

we do not capsize
though the sailors' pipes

go upside down
between their teeth

spraying sparks across the nebulae
from here to you

The air keeps flowing

                                                    11/25

FROM THE ORIGINAL

The first copy from the second copy
was then the third copy from the original

while the original lay back and gazed with
its usual longing at the emerald heavens or

seemed to almost be counting the elusive stars
and some of the more diamond-like galaxies

So the third copy of the original
was then mother to the fourth and fifth

and on down the line spawning copy after copy
which fell into the eager hands and

hearts and minds of the most
avid students while wildfires

raged in the nearby woods and ravenous
mountain lions looked for lunch

This was the master's text that guaranteed
both invisibility and invincibility

against all vicissitudes however fiery or savage
and the copies were needed to cover

the number of needy devotees
closer to the outermost darkness

where one could hear the loud
slithering of snakes

Death lay behind the darkness
but according to the text

endless light lay behind death

and it was urgent for all the most
adept at puzzling out the meanings

to have a copy of the text or a
copy of the copy *ad infinitum*

up to this very poem with its curious notions
as the world goes on combusting

bathed by the
seven oceans

11/26

ON US ALL

A man's tongue and a
woman's cheek

A man's knuckles and a
woman's knees

A man's eagerness and a
woman's reticence

A man's waving arms and a
woman's downward glance

A man's hoarseness in the morning and a
woman's secret tears in the pillow

*(Clouds cover the moon and then a
moment later let it shine)*

It's a desolate landscape when there are
no whispers or cries

Houses between us and the horizon
contain both men and women

both containing themselves and
letting themselves go

Outrageousness kept at a minimum
and outlandishness reserved for special occasions

Yet the nights are generally quiet
and empty streets peaceful

and men lie silently on their backs
and woman lie on their sides

and the morning finds them
Adam and Eve again and their

uncontrollable children some
men some women

with eyes all their own and
hair which slowly turns white

as the sun rises and goes
down again on us all

                                                                  11/27

THE DIVINE PRESENCE

I want to find myself
on the other side of all this

poetry

in The Divine Presence

11/27

ONE MORNING

One morning a man awoke and his
bedroom was full of light

He tore his shirt so the arms were wings
and put pigeons in his shoes so they could fly

The door to his room was a flame of ice
through which he saw the world wobble

and all its voices turn suddenly into
haphazard song

Even cries across fields or vacant lots
were drenched in a musical meaning

So he arose without moving and
the house departed from around him

off on its worldly errands leaving him
prostrate in the direction of his heart

There's no end to this infinite variety of
one single thing this passionate longing

in which our house roofs are full of
prehistoric animals craning their necks

moonward and at the same time
drunken moonlight is falling between

all of us on earth to make us so in
love with that radiance we begin to

dance with it outlining our bodies in
delicious slithery rainbows against

every encroaching dark that might
blast it to smithereens

               11/28

THE WAY ANIMALS LOOK AT US

The way animals look at us
might be the way God looks at us

across open tundras of space and through
constantly showering veils of particles

including our own

But the gaze both personal and
impersonal

loving interest as well as indifference

A gaze as elemental as

fiery explosions on the sun and as
docile as a night full of stars

over the sleeping earth the way a
horse or cat or bird look at us

from their unfathomable centers
in which we are seen

from somewhere beyond us

11/28

A STONE

A stone dropped into a

pond will finally

hit bottom

Love doesn't even know how

lucky it is

to have you

                                                          11/29

OPPOSITE TO THIS ONE

I wonder if there's a sense of procession
a kind of solemnity in
leaving this world behind
going down corridors of gray mist
past those funereal spindly flame cypresses on
either side

alternating their straight dark trunks with spaces of
standing white lions with blank eyes
silent not yawning but at attention
and then white horses between the

trees whose rustling boughs whisper every conversation ever
had by us from childhood to this moment
leaves of words and a coiling light of meanings and
apprehensions as we

walk between them leaving
one populous sea for another

but the sea up ahead a radiant
whirlpool of gentle turning in which we are

whirled out of our bodies at last
and repolished with subtle ones to which
no flesh can compare

entering the one realm in all creation
opposite to this one

11/29

THE GRAND FÊTE

At the Grande Fête everyone's invited to
people start arriving by aerial gondola

Shape-changing twins arrive
dressed in tuxedos

Lady Godiva comes dressed
as a smudge-blotched charwoman

Historians come with inky thumbs
in suits made of parchment

Serenaders arrive on whiffles of song
neon red cummerbunds like those worn at the Vatican

Various woodland creatures arrive
in human disguise and no one's the wiser

Orpheus comes with his head firmly on
wearing a snake costume since

that's what bit Eurydice
and sent her to Hades

(he's trying to reverse it)

Dressmakers priests pompous
diplomats aristocrats

arrive on gold bicycles
with playing cards in the spokes

A forest fire arrives dressed as a fireman
a drought totters in dressed as a skeleton

Even the End of the World
though he's not been invited

dressed as all and everyone
who ever walked the earth

but even wiser
and more beautiful

Then the Next World arrives
not long afterward

wearing the exact same Apocalyptic
costume but in reverse

Conversation bubbles
everyone dances the

standing-still vibrational green dance of
every living thing

Pretty soon distant stars come and
far constellations

Then the Entire Cosmos comes

just before dawn

and at one point *(some say drunk)*
turns inside-out completely

And we all land here as
naked as day

alive at last in a new constitution
ethereally nourished by stream waters

direct from The Source
as well as

bowls of ambrosia and lotus flowers
floating in air

though air is no longer
it's something else altogether

God's Presence taking place
where our place is left vacant

only song
trembling

within reach

among high boughs
of nothingness

12/1

SHOUT OF JOY

A shout of joy goes up and
all is lost

A sob of grief is heard
and day is won

Earth opens up its fissures
while somewhere glide golden birds

Cascades hurl tons of water
while somewhere dies a village of thirst

A tap is heard in the concert hall
and the orchestra bellows

An avalanche roars down a mountainside
and a cricket sings

A song is sung in a jungle
and trees fall

Waves cover over a shipwreck
and silence reigns

We shout and make pretty speeches
while a graveyard snoozes

Everything hardens to a brittle point
while honey oozes

12/2

LOVELY SEXY BEING

1

When I feel my forehead I can feel
the rondure of my skull

and how after I'm dead if I'm
still around I could play

catch with it
tossing it back and forth

2

Will I one day be a
puddle of flesh

exposing the bonework underneath

my organs turned to dust?

This lovely sexy being
I am?

12/4

THE TRUTH IS

The truth is everything this world has to
offer is a disappointment

We're like King Midas in reverse in that
even the gold we touch turns to lead

Desires and pinnacles and even pinnacles of desires
once scaled and reached or reached and collected

turn out to be rag dolls at a storm window being
blown to bits with that blank smile still on them

We must breathe and breed but in this
great department store perhaps our

seeing would best be focused on the
middle distance instead of close up

Even far away would be preferable to the point of
seeing stars and constellations the

sun and moon and their enamored orbits
instead of pulling close to us those

things that are sure to either
dissolve or at some point say *adios* even if

they very softly
close the door behind them

All streets ultimately lead to the sea
and at sea not all boats reach the horizon

Such a cosmos as we are with its
interior weathers and continents might with some

vision and continuous gratitude suffice us
when we see how truly watery this

life is and how truly watery we are
with both trickling through our fingers at the

same rate
at the same time

When the sun's brightest even a hovel's façade
lights up with an almost diamond shine

and when night descends it's all jewels on
black velvet enough for the most dignified

dowager or most charismatic of kings

Rainfall is pearls from heaven spattering on the
emeralds of earth's grassblades and the

secret jades of forests and bushes
that line even poverty's streets

and the air given free for us to breathe is
a long divine outbreath perfectly suitable to our lungs

and the eyesight we're given is enough to
entertain even the most festive of angels hidden in the

shadows or vast spaces between
shadows all around us as we

die one moment and come to life the next
either here or there in the splendid extravagant tent of

God's pure good pleasure and
complete and merciful

satisfaction

                                                                       12/5

JAKE AND THE DESPERADOS

A dangerous group of desperados
came riding into town

just as Mary Elizabeth Louise was
doffing her wedding gown

Her husband Jake was in the bed
waiting for his bride

but Blood Eye Pete and his
gang of four would make him have to decide

which was more important now
with his town at the brink of the fire

the salvation of its few thousand townsfolk
or the fulfillment of his desire

You could hear their twenty hoof beats
from the bedroom where they lay

their guttural shouts and deeper grunts
as they made their desperate way

up Main Street toward Dead Man's Saloon
for a drink or ten of scotch

and it had a way of affecting poor young
Jake in his wedding crotch

He could hear the smashing of glasses and
bodies hitting the floor

so he leapt from the bed and buttoned his
clothes and flew right out the door

leaving Mary Elizabeth Louise against the
pillow like a fragile flower

the beauty mark by her perfect mouth
turning darker and making her dour

But Jake was deputy sheriff and
Sheriff Bart Blank was out of town

And Jake was a conscientious kind of guy
who would never let his people down

He clattered down the stairs in his new wedding boots
and shot out the door to his destiny

repeating verses of the Bible to himself in a
booming heartbeat litany

He'd only been deputy a few days now
as he sauntered down the street to the bar

while Blood Eye Pete and his gang of
four had no respect for his deputy's star

nor star light star bright first star I see

tonight nor star of David nor star of reward

and when Jake burst through those saloon
doors all five swung around toward

poor Jake like wild lions turning on their prey
their bitter claws extended

and it seemed like young newlywed Jake's
life was just about to be ended

The bar became still not a word was uttered
it was silent as a tomb

and suddenly the size of the galaxy
became the size of that smoky room

The bartender's bar-top cloth went
suddenly dry in his shaking hand

and everyone's throats became dry as
well as the six men took their stand

The desperados six feet one or two or
three and in one case six

and Jake a mere five feet eight
saw angel ladders playing tricks

on his focusing eyes and their rainbow
streams to his excited mental cortex

as the picture became increasingly clear
of just how many bodily shipwrecks

we might be counting on the barroom floor
and how much blood might get spilled

when Jake saw the Door of Life open wide
and suddenly saw everything light-filled

and moving in extreme slow-motion showing
expressions of surprise

for instead of desperados before him he now saw
starry spaces before his eyes

Jake came to a sudden stop before them
and by God flung his pistol in the air

where it stayed suspended gun-barrel pointing
at their sudden looks of despair

Blood Eye Pete and the four desperados
drew and shot what was hanging in front of them

but all their bullets came right back at them
for what it was that confronted them

was just their own crazy desperation and
Jake was not even a part of it

and as they all lay dead on the barroom floor

pure silence came back to the heart of it

The stars were perfectly placed back in the
sky and our own Black Hole as well

which is so compacted with deep trapped
light it resembles the depths of Hell

and the vastness of unlimited space
extends past the multiple edges

of everything in existence from distant
planets to wedding cake wedges

And Jake that night achieved fatherhood
with a sweetly realized conception

when he returned to Mary Elizabeth Louise
and her adoring wedding reception

12/10

DELICIOUS LIQUEFACTION OF THE DARK

In the delicious liquefaction of the dark
and relative dissolution of material things

in this heavenly dense center
where only One really matters

and from its high vista all seven
oceans in their languor can be

seen at a glance and all tepid and
torrid rockings of the earth

in whose cradle so many ungrateful swarm
and so few grateful stand and sing

before turning inward to the undertow of the
seas' currents in their unhesitant

sweep and ripple against hardness
and from whose view at the

same time up close and microscopic
populations sidle and slip with fullest

consciousness both of their
source and destination enveloped always by this

deliciousness this dark as edgeless as it is
depthless in its deeps and

blackest in its blackest blacklessness

where His Voice unlicks its splendors

and we shudder to our core

to His central-most

shuddering

12/11

STORMS

A sandstorm blew away the world

A God-storm blew away the sand

                                               12/14

VARIOUS STORIES

There's the story of the headless librarian
and they say she telephoned her
answers to the most often asked questions
such as *"Where is your head?"* or
"Where can I find the section on plumbing?"
And she lived to a ripe old age
and that her voice never quavered

There's the story of the saint's eyebrow
which many said housed a family of sparrows
and at least two generations of chicks
and that the saint went into deep
contemplation while the hatchlings took their first
flying lessons out of the nest

Then there's the tale of the three palominos
who saved the stables from burning down by
swishing their tails with such velocity the
wind literally blew out the flames
and some said they belonged to The
Three Musketeers and others that
they were three of the Four Horses of the
Apocalypse

The stories are unending each more
astonishing than the last each more

aswirl with amazing transformations

such as the cobbler who patched the
king's shoes and found sewn inside an insole a
parchment that revealed the king to be the righteous
cobbler and the cobbler the rightful king

Or the innumerable stories of animals
turning into humans and rabbits
turning into top hats and swans
turning into skies full of flamingos that in turn
fly in a formation that soon becomes a
wedge of bright pink light pointing northwards

and southwards as well as all the
other cardinal points becoming again the
inhalation of God's recreation of this
perfect universe rather like the universal
flood prophet Noah withstood
*(and we with our technical know-how seem
hell bent on re-instigating)*

and the sparkling story of God's
alabaster and golden perfections reduced to the
atoms with which they're composed

and ourselves reduced again at last to call out His
Name and so reconstitute both
ourselves and the endless twice-told stories we are
with all their one-of-a-kind details

under an ever-renewed and
ever renewable sun

12/16

EVERY LABYRINTH

Every labyrinth leads

to the mercy of Allah

                                                                12/24

THE THING ABOUT DEATH

The thing about death is

we've got to let other people
fall around us

and continue falling until

we fall

12/26

THE WORLD

The world loves to put on
representations of itself

Blond wigs and cake makeup are essential
plus massive tummy tucks and unnecessary amputations

Anything to look good
including a few backroom assassinations

With immediate speeches *(in blond wig?)*
of the nation's "going forward" as well as

arresting all wrongdoers who of
course under all those wigs are *yours truly*

Pageants and garish parades
without passing through any makeshift Hoovertowns

who if they appear at all must all
appear miserably happy

The world loves to put out the lights
and turn on the spotlight

focusing on a few recognizable faces
even issuing postage stamps in their honor

(Postage stamps never seem to honor
just the people who use them)

Rabbles and crowds are miniaturized
rebellions and wars romanticized

So the world always ends up looking good
since instead of itself *as itself*

the world loves to put on
representations of itself

> 12/27

OLD BOOT

for Shaykh Hajj Abdal-Haqq Bewley

There's an old boot
battered and raw

It could be Van Gogh's boot
It could be the world

Killed and revived over and over
its sole bent up and its

heel crooked
as if beaten by trees

Traipsed over great clumps in fields
or dodging strafe-fire and

shrapnel
a boot that's seen too much in its

short leathery life
yet soldiers on

brutishly bootish
Presumably for a foot

though it's taken on a life beyond
shoeing something as

ephemeral as a foot
it now seems to fit all feet

and none

More a boat than a boot
More a ship than a shoe

braving earthly waves

Sitting here alone now
beached in a dark brown light

radiantly dark
(it could be God's boot

though God has no foot
nor needs a boot

It's just that it's that kind of boot
No human foot could be so

adorned)

as it sails in
utter stillness

having reached
its end of usefulness

and now will not go anywhere

that is not where it

already is

                                                                12/29

AS IF A WINDSOCK

As if a windsock could tell
which way the spirit is blowing

or a cascade know the exact configuration of
all its falling drops

Just as no statistician can exactly
track where each of us is going

and where our jumpy thoughts will
take us to the interior or to the edge

where smoke rises like corkscrewing
cypresses into a blue bloated sky

and nothing is exactly as it seems

But who has God's true optical gauge?

The leap of wild beasts across a
narrow divide

or an electric shot of lightning that
seems to jag horizontally low to the ground

or a sudden silence in a room full of
people might go some distance

to explaining what it is that so

dazzles and intrigues us onward

in spite of herds of stubborn mules
crossing our path

or our narrow escapes from flash
floods and fire into relatively

normal deliriums where at least the
bobbing faces at our sides and afloat all

around us are angelic in shape
and earnest in their general demeanor

Too much chatter *Pipe down!* and
too much silence *I can't hear you!*

Too much death crowded with
too much life *Back off a little please!*

Go easy on all those seemingly
indiscriminate inclusions

and let some sparrows go from

falling and catch some
falling sparrows in the sweet

benevolence of our hands

A supreme certainty slides up the

straws from all our liquid refreshments

while a supreme indifference looks on the
least of us with tears in its eyes

and none of us goes home alone at
last without at least a

companionable zebra or two or
the shadow of guidance visibly

up ahead who waits for us through every
calamity

and waits around the bend for us
from every

unforeseen disaster

            1/3

WHEN WE DIE

When we die
one world closes and

another snaps open
(Quickly? Gradually? Fogs

dispersing us into it? Or
all at once in perfect focus?) with its

timeliness in its

total lack of time

But *oh!* What
a dimension it is!

How the vistas roll
on and on!

                                                1/4

SPARKS OFF THE MAIN STRIKE

The poem cannot contain it
it contains the poem

Does a waterfall contain its roar
or the roar its waterfall?

Does an elephant contain its swaying
or its lumbering gait contain its elephant?

Do we contain silences between words
or does silence contain us?

And around silence what
contains it?

Sound after which there
is no silence?

Or silence after which
there is no sound?

I began as a tad with big eyes
and did that tad contain me

as I am now
or do I contain that tad?

And our big eyes
Do they contain the world or does the

world contain our eyes and
all they ever see?

And is our sight contained by or
does it contain

all it sees?

In a drop of water
an ocean is contained

And the ocean contains a
single restless drop beating a

single stubborn shore
warmed by sudden sunlight

And what contains light
or does light contain us all?

What light in each of us
can be contained?

A single spark contains night
as night's contained by day

All dark's contained in the
heart of us all

asleep in God's
spark of Light

Sparks

off the Main Strike

1/10

INDEX OF TITLES

19th Poem: The Projector's Beam of Light   44
A Secret Rent in the World   21
A Shout Unheard   169
A Smattering of Conundrums   137
A Stone   180
All Those Poets   26
And Why?   25
Appearance of the Muse   78
As if a Windsock   207
As We Fly Forward   95
Backbent Scribes   23
Beginnings and Endings   109
Blind Samson   123
Blindly Believing   145
Bread Was Butter and Butter Bread   100
Chair   16
Conch Shell   69
Crimson and Scarlet Rivulet Passageways   17
Death Flips a Coin   40
Death Sonnet   55
Deepmost Heartbeat of the World   67
Delicious Liquefaction of the Dark   195
Divine Name   113
Enter the Clowns   166
Eon after Eon   74
Every Labyrinth   200
From the Original   172
Geese Overhead   151
Hounds   80
I Lie Face Down   157
If I Had To Say at This Moment   142

If Our Days are Numbered   85
In All Oracular Song   170
In Broad Daylight   33
Incendiary Air   60
Jake and the Desperados   190
Keyhole   57
Let The Magician   11
Little Door in the Heart   83
Living Flame   140
Locks on Doors   35
Lovely Sexy Being   186
Love's Up Close and Personal Conflagration   124
Lucerne Street at Night   89
Meaning   13
Nothing to Do   128
Nowhere Was Emptiness Unrivered   138
Old Boot   204
Old Man in a Drop of Water   111
On Us All   174
One Morning   177
One Quick Cold Night   131
One Shout   56
Opposite to This One   181
Optical Illusions   149
Orpheus at Rest   104
Paradise Gate   98
Pearl   19
Secretary Bird   31
Seeking and Finding   88
Shadowhood   76
Shout of Joy   185
Silent Stones   163
Skin Deep   29

So Many Things to Say   127
Soap Bubble   14
Some Juggler!   164
Sound the Alarm   27
Sparks Off the Main Strike   211
Stops   103
Storms   197
Superhighway   49
Synopsis of a Nonexistent Trilogy   133
The Desperados   106
The Divine Presence   176
The Doctor's Arrived   101
The Grand Fête   182
The Heavenly Door That is Always Open   91
The Large Caster of Nets   12
The Oyster is in Deep Meditation   121
The Pine Barrens   51
The Practice of Poetry   153
The Sabotage of the Saboteurs   46
The Ship's Captain   53
The Smell of Wet Sackcloth   167
The Thing About Death   201
The Threshold of the Floor   119
The Truth Is   187
The Way Animals Look at Us   179
The Why and the Wherefore   38
The World   202
There's a Sound   71
This Plane's Full of Babies   94
This World   48
To Get to Sleep   160
To the Oneness   158
Treatise on Distortion   62

Until Cockcrow Wake Us   116
Various Stories   198
We Do Things   130
When We Die   210
Whitman   82

ABOUT THE AUTHOR

Born in 1940 in Oakland, California, Daniel Abdal-Hayy Moore's first book of poems, *Dawn Visions*, was published by Lawrence Ferlinghetti of City Lights Books, San Francisco, in 1964, and the second in 1972, *Burnt Heart/Ode to the War Dead*. He created and directed *The Floating Lotus Magic Opera Company* in Berkeley, California in the late 60s, and presented two major productions, *The Walls Are Running Blood*, and *Bliss Apocalypse*. He became a Sufi Muslim in 1970, performed the Hajj in 1972, and has lived and traveled throughout Morocco, Spain, Algeria and Nigeria, landing in California and publishing *The Desert is the Only Way Out*, and *Chronicles of Akhira* in the early 80s (Zilzal Press). Residing in Philadelphia since 1990, in 1996 he published *The Ramadan Sonnets* (Jusoor/City Lights), and in 2002, *The Blind Beekeeper* (Jusoor/Syracuse University Press). He has been the major editor for a number of works, including *The Burdah* of Shaykh Busiri and *The Prayer of the Oppressed*, both translated by Shaykh Hamza Yusuf, and the poetry of Palestinian poet, Mahmoud Darwish, translated by Munir Akash. He is also widely published on the worldwide web: *The American Muslim, DeenPort*, and his own website and poetry blog, among others: www.danielmoorepoetry.com, www.ecstaticxchange.wordpress.com. He has been poetry editor for *Islamica Magazine* and *Seasons Journal,* and a 2010 translation by Munir Akash of *State of Siege*, by Mahmoud Darwish, from Syracuse University Press. The Ecstatic Exchange Series is bringing out the extensive body of his works of poetry (a complete list of published works on page 2).

POETIC WORKS by Daniel Abdal-Hayy Moore
Published and Unpublished

Dawn Visions (published by City Lights, 1964)
Burnt Heart/Ode to the War Dead (published by City Lights, 1972)
This Body of Black Light Gone Through the Diamond (printed by Fred Stone, Cambridge, Mass, 1965)
On The Streets at Night Alone (1965?)
All Hail the Surgical Lamp (1967)
States of Amazement (1970)

Abdallah Jones and the Disappearing-Dust Caper (published by The Ecstatic Exchange/Crescent Series, 2006)
'Ala ud-Deen and the Magic Lamp
The Chronicles of Akhira (1981) (published by Zilzal Press with Typoglyphs by Karl Kempton, 1986)(published in Sparrow on the Prophet's Tomb by The Ecstatic Exchange, 2009)
Mouloud (1984) (A Zilzal Press chapbook, 1995)(published in Sparrow on the Prophet's Tomb by The Ecstatic Exchange, 2009)
Man is the Crown of Creation (1984)
The Look of the Lion (The Parabolas of Sight) (1984)
The Desert is the Only Way Out (completed 4/21/84) (Zilzal Press chapbook, 1985)
Atomic Dance (1984) (am here books, 1988)
Outlandish Tales (1984)
Awake as Never Before (12/26/84) (Zilzal Press chapbook, 1993)
Glorious Intervals (1/1/85) (Zilzal Press chapbook, ?)
Long Days on Earth/Book I (1/28 – 8/30/85)
Long Days on Earth/Book II (Hayy Ibn Yaqzan)
Long Days on Earth/Book III (1/22/86)
Long Days on Earth/Book IV (1986)
The Ramadan Sonnets (Long Days on Earth/Book V) (5/9 – 6/11/86) (Published by Jusoor/City Lights Books, 1996) (Republished as Ramadan Sonnets by The Ecstatic Exchange, 2005)
Long Days on Earth/Book VI (6-8/30/86)
Holograms (9/4/86 – 3/26/87)
History of the World (The Epic of Man's Survival) (4/7 – 6/18/87)

Exploratory Odes (6/25 – 10/18/87)
The Man at the End of the World (11/11 – 12/10/87)
The Perfect Orchestra (3/30 – 7/25/88) (Published by The Ecstatic Exchange, 2009)
Fed from Underground Springs (7/30 – 11/23/88)
Ideas of the Heart (11/27/88 – 5/5/89)
New Poems (scattered poems, out of series, from 3/24 – 8/9/89)
Facing Mecca (5/16 – 11/11/89)
A Maddening Disregard for the Passage of Time (11/17/89 – 5/20/90) (Published by The Ecstatic Exchange, 2009)
The Heart Falls in Love with Visions of Perfection (6/15/90 – 6/2/91)
Like When You Wave at a Train and the Train Hoots Back at You (Farid's Book) (6/11 – 7/26/91) (Published by The Ecstatic Exchange, 2008)
Orpheus Meets Morpheus (8/1/91– 3/14/92)
The Puzzle (3/21/92 – 8/17/93)
The Greater Vehicle (10/17/93 – 4/30/94)
A Hundred Little 3-D Pictures (5/14/94 – 9/11/95)
The Angel Broadcast (9/29 – 12/17/95)
Mecca/Medina Time-Warp (12/19/95 – 1/6/96) (Published as a Zilzal Press chapbook, 1996)(published in Sparrow on the Prophet's Tomb by The Ecstatic Exchange, 2009)
Miracle Songs for the Millennium (1/20 – 10/16/96)
The Blind Beekeeper (11/15/96 – 5/30/97) (Published 2002 by Jusoor/Syracuse University Press)
Chants for the Beauty Feast (6/3 – 10/28/97)
You Open a Door and it's a Starry Night (10/29/97 – 5/23/98) (Published by The Ecstatic Exchange, 2009)
Salt Prayers (5/29 – 10/24/98) (Published by The Ecstatic Exchange, 2005)
Some (10/25/98 – 4/25/99)
Flight to Egypt (5/1 – 5/16/99)
I Imagine a Lion (5/21 – 11/15/99) (Published by The Ecstatic Exchange, 2006)
Millennial Prognostications (11/25/99 – 2/2/2000) (Published by the Ecstatic Exchange, 2009)
Shaking the Quicksilver Pool (2/4 – 10/8/2000) (Published by The Ecstatic Exchange, 2009)
Blood Songs (10/9/2000 – 4/3/2001)
The Music Space (4/10 – 9/16/2001) (Published by The Ecstatic Exchange, 2007)

Where Death Goes (9/20/2001 – 5/1/2002) (Published by The Ecstatic Exchange, 2009)
The Flame of Transformation Turns to Light (99 Ghazals Written in English) (5/14 – 8/21/2002) (Published by The Ecstatic Exchange, 2007)
Through Rose-Colored Glasses (7/22/2002 – 1/15/2003) (Published by The Ecstatic Exchange, 2007)
Psalms for the Broken-Hearted (1/22 – 5/25/2003) (Published by The Ecstatic Exchange, 2006)
Hoopoe's Argument (5/27 – 9/18/03)
Love is a Letter Burning in a High Wind (9/21 – 11/6/2003) (Published by The Ecstatic Exchange, 2006)
Laughing Buddha/Weeping Sufi (11/7/2003 – 1/10/2004) (Published by The Ecstatic Exchange, 2005)
Mars and Beyond (1/20 – 3/29/2004) (Published by The Ecstatic Exchange, 2005)
Underwater Galaxies (4/5 – 7/21/2004) (Published by The Ecstatic Exchange, 2007)
Cooked Oranges (7/23/2004 – 1/24/2005 (Published by The Ecstatic Exchange, 2007)
Holiday from the Perfect Crime (1/25 – 6/11/2005)
Stories Too Fiery to Sing Too Watery to Whisper (6/13 – 10/24/2005)
Coattails of the Saint (10/26/2005 – 5/10/2006) (Published by The Ecstatic Exchange, 2006)
In the Realm of Neither (5/14 – 11/12/06) (Published by The Ecstatic Exchange, 2008)
Invention of the Wheel (11/13/06 – 6/10/07) (Published by The Ecstatic Exchange, 2010)
The Sound of Geese Over the House (6/15 – 11/4/07)
The Fire Eater's Lunchbreak (11/11/07 – 5/19/2008) (Published by The Ecstatic Exchange, 2008)
Sparks Off the Main Strike (5/24/2008 – 1/10/2009) (Published by The Ecstatic Excange, 2010)
Stretched Out on Amethysts (1/13 – 9/17/2009) (Published by The Ecstatic Exchange, 2010)
The Throne Perpendicular to All that is Horizontal (9/18/09 – 1/25/10)
In Constant Incandescence (2/10 – 8/13/10)
The Caged Bear Spies the Angel (8/30/10 –)

www.ingramcontent.com/pod-product-compliance
Lightning Source LLC
Chambersburg PA
CBHW032042150426
43194CB00006B/390